PARENTS TEENS AND BOUNDARIES

How To Draw the Line

JANE BLUESTEIN, PH.D.

Health Communications, Inc.
Deerfield Beach, Florida

Library of Congress Cataloging-in-Publication Data

Bluestein, Jane.
   Parents, teens, and boundaries / Jane Bluestein.
      p.   cm.
   Includes bibliographic references.
   ISBN 1-55874-279-4
   1. Parent and teenager. 2. Parenting. 3. Communication in
   the family. I. Title.
HQ799.15.B58   1993   93-13942
306.874—dc20   CIP

©1993 Jane Bluestein
ISBN 1-55874-279-4

Publisher: Health Communications, Inc.
                 3201 S.W. 15th Street
                 Deerfield Beach, Florida 33442-8190

Cover design by Robert Cannata

Dedication

To my parents,
their parents and all parents
who did the best they could
with what they had.

Acknowledgements

I owe a tremendous debt of gratitude to the following people who are very much a part of this project:

To the countless parents I've encountered in my presentations — and airplanes, restaurants and hotel lobbies — who have graciously allowed me to share their stories and examples.

To Barbara Nichols, who encouraged me to show up in whatever ways my energy and personality have emerged in my writing.

To Nathaniel Branden and LeRoy Foster, for verbalizing their support when and where it counted.

To my WISE friends — my immediate network of Women in Self-Esteem, which includes Gail Dusa, Ginger Lambert, Louise Hart, Peggy Bielen and Shirley Backles — who encouraged me to do this book and celebrated with me when it was finished.

To my sister, Susanna Bluestein, whose continual unfolding and unrelenting love for the truth never ceases to inspire me.

To my teachers, healers and friends whose unconditional love, patience and generosity of spirit have allowed me to finally experience myself from much the same place. My love, blessings and gratitude to Terri Wollett, Joy Jacobson, Maurine Renville, Biker Steve, Kathy Jenkins, Gretchen Silver, Andy Quinones, Sue Harden, Debby Hartz, Debra Sugar, Aili Pogust, Susan Stiger, Kathy Hayes, Judy Lawrence, Nancy Knickerbocker, Kathy Morey, Lynn Collins, Richard Biffle, Glynda, Mommom and the many friends of Lois and Bill W.

To my husband, Jerry Tereszkiewicz, whose mere existence in my life makes everything better.

And to Spirit for all of the above.

Contents

Preface

A Note About Wants And Needs

By some definitions, I use the term "needs" rather loosely in this book. When I talk about needs, whether kids' or parents' needs, I'm referring to something that is wanted, desired or required. I've got a couple of dictionaries that will back me up, but there are those who insist that the only real needs we have are oxygen, food and water; everything else is a "want."

Well, okay. If your goal is simply survival, I suppose that's true. But most of us are reaching beyond survival, and certainly we want more for the children in our lives. Therefore, oxygen, food and water are simply not enough. Necessary, yes. But once those basic needs are met, it's time to start looking at a few other needs, such as belonging, emotional safety, success, dignity and empowerment. In terms of personal development, these are far more than just "wants."

I have tried to avoid the vernacular use of the word, as in "I *need* the car Saturday" or "I *need* to have this ironed," although I do find these uses acceptable in context.

Perhaps it would help to think in terms of higher- or lower-level needs, some of which will certainly be subject to individual value systems. But regardless of our personal orientation to this particular word, let's try to keep the issues in focus: building healthy family relationships that encourage love, cooperation and self-care.

In my book that's something we all **need.**

PART I

YOUR RELATIONSHIP WITH YOUR TEENS

The Relationship: Your Teenager And You

THE STORIES

Kim has a 15-year-old son with lots of freedom and few responsibilities. When friends reply to Kim's frustration with the suggestion of a few ground rules, Kim throws up her hands and says, "He won't listen to me. What can I do? He's bigger than I am. It's just easier if I do it all myself."

Glynda has a pretty good relationship with her three teenagers. "My only complaint is the den. It's the main room of the house. We all use it. I can't stand it being a mess, but I seem to be the only one who feels that way. It seems the only time anyone pitches in is when I'm on the verge of flipping out about it."

Bob's daughter, Celine, seems to be in a state of constant conflict with her English teacher. Bob has talked to Celine. He's talked to the teacher and the school counselor and the vice principal. "I just don't know what else I can do about this," he laments.

Marie looks at her son and shakes her head. "Do you believe that hair? I am so embarrassed for anyone to see him like that."

Debby and Joe adore their daughter Kristi. Usually a fairly reliable kid, Kristi has been rather irresponsible with the use of the family car lately. Although Debby and Joe have repeatedly threatened to revoke her privileges, they gave in and loaned her the car again this weekend. "After all," they explain, "this *is* the big game."

Alan always felt close to his son. "Suddenly Chris hit adolescence and I hardly know him. He really used to share a lot, but now I can barely get one-word answers out of him. I feel completely shut out of his life."

CHANGING KIDS

Talk to the parents of any teenager and this is what you're likely to hear: concern, frustration, anger, anguish, sadness, fear. Previously cooperative kids suddenly become rebellious and rude. Once accessible children now seem remote. In some instances, you'll hear about kids who were once easy to control but are now taking the upper hand.

What's wrong here? These parents love their kids and want healthy, functional relationships with them. Why do so many parents dread this time in their children's lives? And why do so many parent-child relationships falter at this stage of the game?

The examples above represent a variety of the ways in which boundary issues can interfere with relationships. Boundaries are anything marking a limit and are essential for all healthy relationships. They represent the conditions under which we will participate, or continue to participate, in some activity: "I will drive you to the mall *as soon as* your room is clean." Or they may represent the conditions under which you will allow, to the degree that you are able, some activity to occur or continue: "You can have the car again next weekend *as long as* you return it by the time we agreed on."

Sometimes called contingencies, sometimes called rules, boundaries are what we use to take care of ourselves in relationships with others and how we try to maintain some order and sanity in our lives. In the absence of boundaries, we can do some pretty crazy things to one another — and allow others to do some pretty crazy things to us.

In many of the examples of conflict that parents have shared with me, we've been able to trace the source of the conflict to a lack of boundaries *somewhere*. Either the parent failed to set boundaries, didn't maintain or enforce boundaries that had been expressed or violated a child's boundaries. When we talk about the need for boundaries, the parents, educators and even the counselors frequently aren't sure what we're talking about.

Because boundaries are so emphatically about self-care, and because self-care is often a foreign concept in our culture, this basic relationship skill tends to fall by the wayside in our individual growth and development.

The Challenge Of Setting Boundaries

Few of us are especially adept at setting boundaries with anyone, and for good reason.

BOUNDARY BACKGROUNDS

- When you were growing up, were you told that other people's needs were more important than yours?
- Were you rewarded for self-sacrificing and people-pleasing?
- Were you taught to obey and then shamed, hurt or punished if you didn't?
- Were you scolded for questioning authority?
- Were you taught to avoid conflict at any cost?
- Were you often told that you were responsible for someone else's feelings or behaviors?

If you answer yes to most of these questions, the price was your sense of self, the foundation for setting boundaries.

Was your privacy respected? Was it okay to have your own feelings and opinions? Were you encouraged to solve your own problems and supported through the process, or was someone always there to tell you what to do? Or did you spend too much time fending for yourself, perhaps taking care of other family members with very little support? These experiences, too, influenced your sense of where you end and where others begin.

How do you typically respond to conflict? If your pattern is either one of rebellion or one of compliance, you probably haven't had much practice setting boundaries.

As a child, did you experience verbal, physical, emotional or sexual abuse? It's hard to develop boundaries when any part of your self, including your dignity and sense of worth, is violated.

Clearly, Boundary-Setting 101 is not typically a part of a child's education. If anything, most of us have been conditioned *not* to set boundaries as a way to avoid the negative reactions of others. The ability to set boundaries to take care of ourselves begins with the belief that the "self" is worth caring for. If we've learned that taking care of ourselves results in conflict, rejection or abandonment, it's likely that we'll shut down when we need to set a boundary, rather than take that risk.

In addition, for most of us, there has been a severe shortage of healthy role models. Most of the adults in our lives tend to fall into one of two categories: bulldozers or doormats.

Bulldozers

Bulldozers appear to take care of themselves, but their version of self-care does not take other people's needs into consideration. Bulldozers need to win and feel entitled to do so at the expense of the other person.

This is not boundary-setting. Boundary-setting considers the needs of the other person, although it does not always accommodate them. In other words, "My way or the highway" is bulldozing, not boundary-setting.

Doormats

Doormats function as though they have no boundaries. They are agreeable, nice and fine. (At least until their resentment builds up to one nasty tolerance break, which can make the meanest Bulldozer look pretty tame.) Doormats are terribly accommodating, but do so at the expense of their own needs. They tend to be on the losing end of most conflicts. However, by not sticking up for themselves, they not only avoid many conflicts, they also appear to look good, feel self-righteous and validate a self-perception of helplessness and victimization. There's a great payoff for being a Doormat, but there's also a high price to pay in loss of self.

Clearly these patterns have nothing to do with boundary-setting, although Doormats often hope that being "nice" enough will inspire people to recognize their needs and accommodate them. However, true boundary-setting always takes one's own needs into account and relies on honest and direct communication rather than manipulation and clairvoyance.

Growing up with these models, we receive a number of messages that create obstacles when we attempt to take care of ourselves in relationships with others, messages that connect our worth and lovableness to our ability to please others. If most of the people in our early lives operated on some form of win-lose method of conflict resolution, either by violating and disempowering (as a Bulldozer) or by self-abandoning (as a Doormat), we can hardly imagine win-win solutions that consider the needs of all people involved.

OTHERS' REACTIONS

In the process of establishing healthy belief systems and behaviors, our progress can be set back seriously by the reactions of others, especially if we have a history of people-pleasing. If most of our friends and family members are used to seeing us as caretakers with no clear sense of boundaries, who place higher priorities on other people's needs than our own, they will certainly respond in whatever ways seem necessary to maintain the status quo. One woman lamented, "I've tried setting boundaries, but my parents get hurt, my husband gets mad and my kids feel abandoned. What's the use?"

What's the use indeed? People do what works and our loved ones can become fairly aggressive when old tactics fail them. By the same token, we can take drastic measures when our self-protection becomes important enough. One friend got so tired of her grown children showing up on her doorstep with all of their kids and possessions that she finally sold her house and bought a one-bedroom apartment to make it crystal clear that *moving home* was simply no longer an option.

Perhaps you'll find success with less extreme options, but I believe that the greatest contributions any of us can make to a relationship is a healthy sense of self. And that means doing whatever it takes.

OLD MESSAGES/NEW MESSAGES

The following lists some of the "old" and familiar messages children receive in their dealings with adults, both in their families and, for the most part, in the educational system. There follows some alternatives to these messages that reflect a belief system that will support self-care and boundary-setting.

Old Messages	New Messages
If only my kids/spouse/boss/parents would change, my life would be better.	If my current behaviors aren't working, I am willing to change them.
Other people's actions, words and attitudes create my feelings and determine my behaviors, words and attitudes.	My *reactions* to other people's actions, words and attitudes create my feelings. I am responsible for my feelings and actions.
This is just the way I am.	I always have choices about my own behavior, language and attitudes.
Sometimes you have to act angry, helpless or sad in order to get people	

to do what you want.	I avoid using my feelings to try to change other people.
I am responsible for my children's behavior, appearance and performance.	I can guide, reflect and support my children and still leave them responsible for their own behavior.
My house, my rules.	We all live here together. While I may have the final say in a lot of situations, their needs and feelings always matter.
When other people hurt or disappoint me, I have the right to hurt them back or try to make them feel guilty.	I can take care of myself without deliberately hurting or manipulating others.
If you really loved me, you'd put my needs first.	Self-abandonment is not really loving behavior. Take care of yourself.
I will do my best to take care of others. If they're happy, I'm happy.	I will do my best to take care of myself and still consider other people's needs and feelings.
It's important that other people have high opinions of me.	What others think of me is none of my business.
I don't care how you treat me as long as you love me and never leave.	I don't care if you love me, just treat me right. (Or: I will not tolerate abusive behavior, no matter how you say you feel about me.)
Peace at any price.	I am willing to risk conflict and even abandonment in order to take care of myself.

If the "new" messages characterize the way you operate in relation to others, your relationships are probably pretty healthy, although probably not conflict-free. If the old messages are all too familiar, chances are you're experiencing stresses in your relationships that could be minimized or even eliminated. There *is* a better way.

These new messages may sound foreign, frightening or even impossible at first. Hang in there. This book tells what the new messages look like when you translate them into specific parent-child interactions. There *are* things you can do to build healthy relationships, even if you currently stand firmly rooted in the old messages.

EXERCISE

The following questions can help you examine the experiences that have contributed to your parenting practices and beliefs.

As you were growing up, in what ways were you *encouraged* to set and maintain boundaries, particularly with regard to: Your space and belongings (privacy, your room, drawers/closets, diaries, etc.)?

_____

_____

Your problems?

_____

_____

Your feelings?

_____

_____

Your body?

_____

_____

Your opinions?

_____

_____

Your preferences and needs?

_____

_____

Other people's needs?

_____

_____

How have these experiences affected the way you treat your children?

_____

_____

As you were growing up, in what ways were you *discouraged* from setting and maintaining boundaries, particularly with regard to: Your space and belongings (privacy, your room, drawers/closets, diaries, etc.)?

_____

_____

_____

Your problems?

_____

_____

Your feelings?

_____

_____

Your body?

_____

_____

Your opinions?

_____

_____

Your preferences and needs?

_____

_____

Other people's needs?

_____

_____

How have these experiences affected the way you treat your children?

_____

_____

Which of the "old" messages were particularly familiar to you?

_____

_____

In what ways have these "old" messages affected your parenting behavior?

_____

_____

Which of the "new" messages were particularly familiar to you?

_____

_____

In what ways have these "new" messages affected your parenting behavior?

_____

_____

Three

Setting Boundaries With Teenagers

If you don't have much experience setting boundaries before you have children, becoming a parent will not automatically endow you with that ability. And yet it quickly becomes very obvious that all families need boundaries in order to operate. Children need limits so that they can feel safe and secure; and they are able to grow and learn by testing these limits.

As far as setting these boundaries, we tend to imitate our models — usually our own parents — despite our best intentions. Sure, you probably don't have a problem being a win-win, even-handed, democratic parent when the kids are doing what you want. But it's a sure bet that you'll become the worst of both of your own parents the first time junior loses it in the grocery store.

One possible solution is to become the exact opposite of the adults you were surrounded with as a child, which is usually just as destructive. For example, parents who grew up with too many limits, who remember the pain of feeling disempowered, deprived or simply smothered, may go to the opposite extreme and impose too few limits. These parents confuse loving behavior with permissiveness. The difference is boundaries: loving behavior requires them, permissiveness ignores them.

More often than not, these parents tend to swing between the two extremes, which is crazy-making for all concerned. One mother shared her resistance to setting any boundaries with her kids: "I feel like I'm cramping their self-expression and creativity when I say no. I love these kids and want them to be happy, to have things I never had. So I have a tendency to be overindulgent. And yet at the first sign of misbehavior, I lash out because I resent the fact that they don't appreciate all I've done for them." Indeed, finding some sanity between their needs and one's own is one of the greatest challenges of any relationship between adults and kids.

CHANGING NEEDS

Children's needs keep changing as they grow. It's developmentally normal for kids to attempt to separate from their parents at various stages in their growth. Parental control — or the illusion of control — typically diminishes as children get older, and the limits that are necessary to keep young children safe and secure become less restrictive as they become more independent. Sometimes it's hard to keep up, especially during adolescence, when your child can be adultlike one minute and infantile the next.

Often conflicts arise because kids' boundaries keep shifting. Where it may once have been necessary and appreciated, your involvement and advice — or even your mere existence — may suddenly be perceived as intrusive. Your kids are now drawing lines where none existed before, and you may find yourself in a constant game of "catch-up," while still needing to re-examine, re-establish and re-assert boundaries of your own.

Because your kids keep changing, parenting strategies that once worked beautifully can suddenly be ineffective.

Kids who once thrived on your approval are now far more interested in the approval of their peers. All your limits, values and opinions that have normally been respected will now be challenged, even in the healthiest families.

In win-lose relationships, this will be even more obvious. For example, if your relationship has been fairly authoritarian (win-lose, with your child on the losing end), as an adolescent your child has the resources, and even the physical size, to turn that around. The same is true of permissiveness: if you've been operating without limits, you're due for a break in tolerance by the time your children hit adolescence, if you haven't already had several.

Kids do what works. If whining, pouting, tantrums or similar behaviors have inspired you to cave in on your boundaries, change your mind about the limits you set or quit bothering altogether, it's likely that these tactics will only become more extreme and sophisticated as time goes on.

Expectations

Expectations are a part of the picture, too, especially when the reality of a child's behavior doesn't match the picture you have of how he *should* be acting. Suddenly you see this child in a much more grown-up body and imagine, perhaps, that his emotional growth has followed suit. Unfortunately, sensibility and maturity rarely emerge with all those adolescent hormones and all the "shoulds" in the world won't change that. Furthermore, adolescent behavior can be remarkably inconsistent, and a moment's lapse into apparent responsibility doesn't necessarily portend instant adulthood.

If your expectations simply reflect your value system, you may get into trouble because the picture you have of who your kids should be is probably different from theirs. Expecting your child to make the football team, the dean's list and the country's best law school can create a lot of conflict with a kid who hates sports, is satisfied with academic survival and aspires to a career on MTV.

Enmeshment

This brings up the issue of enmeshment: it's hard to set boundaries with people if you can't separate yourself from them. Are you reasonably clear about where you end and where your child begins? To what degree do you see your daughter as an individual, separate from yourself? How much of your serenity and self-esteem depend on her behavior, appearance or achievement? Can you appreciate the possibility that some areas of her life may be unrelated to you, different from you or even (gulp!) none of your business? Would she rate your level of involvement in her life as uncomfortable and inappropriate? In what instances might he be right?

"Jerkiness"

And finally there is the widely held belief that kids, at this age, are generally jerks. Fortunately some parents would disagree, but if a kid ever has a tendency toward "jerkiness," chances are it will be during this time.

If rearing your children has been difficult for you to handle as they were growing up, you might be in for a rough few years now. As they struggle to manage the physical and social changes they are going through, they will probably go through some phases of strangeness. Perhaps you need to examine your intolerance, talk it over with other parents or get outside advice. Kids need help, not judgment, at this crucial stage of development and occasional "jerk" behavior is normal and perhaps even healthy as they explore ways to become an adult.

The teen years offer terrific opportunities for your relationship to deepen and grow in some wonderful ways. But as in any relationship, an essential enhancement tool is the boundary.

How Do You Parent?

Let's examine your current parenting patterns and values. In each pair of statements, mark the one you identify with most strongly, the one that "feels" most like you.

_____ I explain what I want from my child.
_____ My child should know what I want by now.

_____ "You'll know your room is clean when the following five things are done . . ."
_____ "Get upstairs and clean your room."

_____ "What do you need to do about that?"
_____ "Here's what you need to do about that."

_____ We have immediate consequences for misbehavior and broken agreements.
_____ I frequently give my child warnings and reminders when he misbehaves or forgets to follow through on agreements.

_____ My child is capable of resolving conflicts with her friends.

_____ I often have to talk to my child's friends (or their parents) when conflicts arise.

_____ My child is capable of resolving conflicts with his teachers.

_____ I often have to talk to my child's teachers (or the administrators) when conflicts arise.

_____ "Let's watch this movie together when you finish the dishes."

_____ "Would you please wash the dishes for me?"

_____ I want my child to care about me.

_____ I don't care if my child likes me as long as she respects me.

_____ "I've identified ten things that need to be done around the house every week. We'll pass the list around so we can each choose two."

_____ "I've identified ten things that need to be done around the house every week. Here are the two you need to do."

_____ I want my child to cooperate with me.

_____ I want my child to obey me.

_____ I respect the fact that my child has different tastes than I do.

_____ I am often embarrassed by my child's tastes.

_____ I may not accept my child's misbehavior (or poor choices), but I can always accept my child.

_____ I find it difficult to accept my child if he misbehaves (or makes a poor choice).

_____ I want my child to cooperate with me and I show my appreciation when she does.

_____ I want my child to cooperate with me and I punish him when he doesn't.

_____ My child can choose responsibly and still not choose what I would like.

_____ I am reluctant to let my child make decisions because she may not choose what I would like.

_____ I allow my child to experience the natural consequences of his poor choices.

_____ I frequently rescue my child from the consequences of his poor choices.

_____ I can support my child's independent problem-solving without doing it for him or telling him what to do.

_____ My advice and intervention are necessary to help my child solve problems.

_____ If my child breaks an agreement, she loses that privilege for a specified period of time.

_____ If my child breaks an agreement, she can retain that privilege as long as she has a good excuse.

_____ It is possible to meet a child's need for power within limits that do not hurt or disempower anyone else.

_____ Give them an inch and they'll take a yard.

_____ I am willing to work for my child's respect.

_____ My child should respect me because I am his parent.

_____ I believe my child is entitled to the same kind of respect, space, privacy and power that I want.

_____ My child can have those things when she gets her own house.

_____ I enjoy my kid most of the time.

_____ I don't enjoy my kid most of the time.

_____ "Keep your soccer equipment off the steps so no one trips over it."

_____ "Keep your soccer equipment off the steps because I said so."

_____ My kid can manage okay even if I'm not there.

_____ I cringe at the thought of leaving my kid alone.

_____ "This room needs to be picked up before dinner!"
_____ "You are such an inconsiderate slob!"

_____ My child is allowed to express his feelings — including anger, sadness and fear.
_____ I try to discourage my child from feeling those things.

_____ When my child is upset, I can support her without interfering with her feelings.
_____ When my child is upset, I believe I should try to cheer her up.

_____ "Your report card is terrific! All that hard work certainly paid off."
_____ "I'm so proud of you when you get good grades!"

_____ "As soon as you finish your homework, you can come down and watch TV."
_____ "You are not turning on that TV until your homework is done."

_____ I ask my kid to help plan meals.
_____ I decide on what we eat here.

_____ I spend time talking and doing things with my kid every day.
_____ I hardly ever see my kid.

_____ My kid finds cooperation personally rewarding.
_____ My kid cooperates to please me (or avoid my anger).

_____ Everyone works better when there is a meaningful payoff.
_____ A kid should not have to be rewarded for doing what he is supposed to do.

_____ I can feel like a successful parent even if my child makes dumb choices.
_____ I can feel like a successful parent as long as my child cooperates (and doesn't embarrass me).

_____ I am flexible and willing to change my own behavior to improve my relationship with my child.

_____ If only my child would shape up, we'd have a great relationship.

_____ I attempt to work out solutions with my child that would allow us both to win.

_____ Negotiating with a child only encourages him to take advantage of you.

_____ I have clear positive goals for myself as a parent.

_____ I just want to minimize conflict and embarrassment.

_____ I accept and validate my child's feelings.

_____ My child is simply too sensitive.

_____ "If you get your clothes in the hamper by Friday, I'll be happy to wash them."

_____ "I feel angry when you don't put your clothes in the hamper."

_____ I frequently tell my child that I love her.

_____ I am uncomfortable saying "I love you" to my child.

_____ "You can resume your telephone privileges as soon as you come up with a plan that will guarantee that I'll get my messages."

_____ "I've had it! How many times do I have to tell you to take a message when somebody calls for me?"

_____ I attempt to focus on the positive aspects of my child's behavior.

_____ How will a child learn without "constructive" criticism?

_____ I value and encourage my child's opinions.

_____ A child should respect authority. It is disrespectful to challenge an adult's opinions.

_____ I encourage my child's independence.

_____ I feel threatened by my child's independence.

_____ I am able to meet my own needs and feel happy and successful, independent of my child.

_____ My happiness depends on my child's ability to make positive, constructive choices.

Like the "new messages" in the previous list, the first statement in each pair reflects the philosophy expressed in this book. If you have identified most strongly with these statements, this book will reinforce and enhance what you're already doing.

The second statement in each pair reflects a less healthy model, characterized by a win-lose orientation and various unresolved co-dependency issues. If you find these statements more strongly characterize your relationship with your kids, you're in good company. This is the way most of us learned to interact with one another.

If you had trouble deciding between the two statements, or even in seeing a difference in some cases, the following chapters will compare these parenting styles which are very different and generally exclusive of one another.

Five

A Note About All-Or-Nothing Thinking

One of the greatest obstacles to effective parenting, and indeed to personal growth in general, is a nasty little habit called "all-or-nothing thinking" (sometimes called black-and-white thinking). This tendency surfaces in relation to certain issues.

For example, the parents I've worked with have been unanimous in not wanting their kids to be people-pleasers, especially when someone pressures them to do something illegal or potentially dangerous. They know that people-pleasers simply *can't* "just say no." And yet, there is a certain amount of apprehension in admitting this. The reason: all-or-nothing thinking. When people start worrying about their kids as people-pleasers, they wonder whether they have to choose between raising Mother Teresa or Jack the Ripper.

Not so. Look at Table 5.1 and you'll see there is an alternative. If your perception of your teens — and your role as a parent — is colored by all-or-nothing thinking, you may believe that your options are limited to either encouraging compliance or tolerating rebelliousness. While Table 5.1 offers a rather simplified illustration of kids with these tendencies, it also reveals a third option, one that most parents find preferable.

POWER ISSUES

All-or-nothing thinking also comes up with power issues. Many of us believe that the only way we can maintain any control in our relationships is to control the *people* in those relationships, especially if those people are children. These parents see a child's developmentally-normal need to influence and control his own life as a threat to their authority. If the parents believe that "either this kid has power or I do," power struggles are certain to ensue. (Why do you think everyone calls two-year-olds "terrible"?) So it's understandable that when parenting "experts" talk about *empowering* kids, parents get nervous. In a win-lose, all-or-nothing context this can't even begin to make sense. Black-or-white thinking doesn't allow for boundaries that require teens to function without disempowering anyone else.

Even the idea of boundaries is sure to bring up some all-or-nothing thinking. If you've learned to equate words like "nice," "good" or "dependable," for example, with never saying no, always doing what's expected of you and putting everyone else first, the idea of setting boundaries may suggest that you're going to become the exact opposite. If you typically deny yourself privacy, space or time to be alone because "someone might need me," or if you frequently hear yourself saying things like, "Well, if I don't do it, nobody will," you may be harboring a nagging sense that the world is going to fall apart completely if you set a boundary that might prevent you from holding it together.

Those of us who have learned to aspire to being indispensable, whose "niceness" and worth depend upon it, have paid a high price. By becoming responsible for others, our sense of self gets lost. This is why boundaries are so important. That's why it's equally important to have some alternative to seeing our choices only as either being indispensable or being unreliable, unhelpful and basically useless.

HEALTHY INTERDEPENDENCY

The first time a friend of mind heard of co-dependency she said, "Well, if that means I can't be nice to anyone, I'd rather be co-dependent." When we can get beyond the limits of all-or-nothing thinking, we can see the difference between co-dependency and healthy *inter*dependency, between self-abandonment and being considerate or between disempowering and setting boundaries. We can see that being responsible *to* others is not the same, nor nearly as exhausting, as being responsible *for* others. We can see that self-caring people are not necessarily selfish and that parents don't have to make kids lose in order to win.

Try to imagine an alternative to the extremes of all-or-nothing thinking. We may not have much practice at it, but, for the sake of all our relationships, it is truly time to learn how to run down the middle.

Table 5.1

Options Available With All-Or-Nothing Thinking		An Alternative
Behavior	Rebellious/ disobedient.	Compliant/ obedient.	Cooperative.
Descriptor	Self-centered.	Self-abandoning.	Self-caring.
Focus	My needs.	Your needs.	My needs and yours.
Goal	Having my own way no matter what; power; being left alone.	Avoiding conflict and abandonment; approval.	Getting what I want with a minimum of conflict and inconvenience for others.

Options Available With All-Or-Nothing Thinking		An Alternative
Responsibility Someone else's fault; sees little connection between behavior and outcomes.	"Just following orders"; disempowered; sees self as having few choices.	Responsible for own behavior; sees self as having choices and power.
Power play Uses power to disempower; win-lose.	Gives power away; lose-win.	Shares power; win-win.
Power tools Anger, violence, passive-aggressiveness; secrecy, isolation.	Being "nice", being perfect, doing what everyone expects; achievement, recognition; tears, guilt; passive-aggressiveness.	Negotiating, compromise; ability to identify personal needs; self-expression; ability to make you a deal you can't refuse.
Feelings Difficulty expressing feelings in constructive, non-violating ways.	Feelings are frequently "stuffed" and/or denied; vulnerable to tolerance breaks, can be explosive.	Not necessary to use feelings to manipulate, hurt or control; can express in nonhurtful ways.
Costs Relationships.	Sense of self, self-worth.	May create conflict with authoritarian or manipulative people. Can threaten, upset or alienate people with weak or no boundaries.
Stays safe by Not needing you, not caring.	Keeping you happy (so you won't criticize or leave).	Identifying and expressing needs; taking care of self. (Probably feels pretty safe to begin with.)
Boundaries Few, as far as others are concerned.	Few, as far as self is concerned.	Has personal boundaries; respects others' boundaries.

What Do You Want?

Most of the parents I've encountered in my work want pretty much the same things from and for their children. In general they hope to have children who are cooperative, responsible, contributing members of the family, kids who are able to think and function independently, and kids who are, for the most part, decent, considerate human beings.

How these desires are lived out differs from one family to the next. Responsible behavior in one family may simply involve doing the dishes occasionally; in another, it means something along the lines of winning a Nobel Prize. The point is, most people who live in families want to do so with a maximum of cooperation and a minimum of conflict. We want to know that at some point our children will be able to function as happy, productive members of the world at large, without us at their sides.

WHAT DO IDEAL CHILDREN LOOK LIKE?

What do ideal children look like in your mind? How would you describe the best of all possible relationships you could have with your kids? What kind of a parent would you like to be? These questions are very important because you need to keep looking at how your behaviors either reinforce or undermine these goals.

Another very important question is: Are the models we have for parenting getting us the results we want? If your kids are less than cooperative, are vulnerable to peer pressure and other people's approval and have a hard time functioning independently in healthy, constructive ways, then maybe the models need changing. For the most part, what we've learned and what we do in our relationships with our kids can actually sabotage our parenting goals and encourage the exact opposite behaviors.

Look at that self-assessment in Chapter 4. The first statement in each pair reflects the kind of parenting behavior that actually does teach independent problem-solving and self-caring behavior. Yet most people find the second statement in each pair to be far more consistent with their parenting behaviors. Despite the positive outcomes we'd like to inspire, these behaviors tend to reinforce dependency, people-pleasing, the need to shut down emotionally to feel safe and the need to rebel to feel powerful. What parent wants that? Unfortunately, if these are the only tools at our disposal, it's hard to get a better result.

It's always going to be easier to settle for positive outcomes at the expense of process, but consider the cost in the long run. Raising a people-pleaser doesn't sound good on paper, but who isn't tempted to shoot for that goal if the people being "pleased" include you? If your relationship looks as if it's working okay — and that's probably exactly how it looks if your children aren't too obnoxious or in too much trouble — then change may seem like a lot of work for nothing. Most of us resist change even at our most desperate moments. So why rock the boat if the water looks calm?

TRUSTING THE PROCESS

In the short run, restructuring relationships can indeed create conflict and confusion. While some techniques can inspire immediate positive change (with some of the children, some of the time), others require more time, persistence and patience. If your relationship is in serious trouble, it will take a while to rebuild trust — on all sides. Hang in there. Trust the process and the desired outcome may happen.

Over time, developing healthy relationships with kids can pay off handsomely for all concerned. Strategies for change are probably well worth a second look because healthy relationships with your kids can help them learn to solve problems and express feelings without hurting others. Healthy relationships reduce the potential for addictive, compulsive and destructive behaviors; they provide the groundwork for long-term caring relationships with you and others in their lives.

EXERCISE

The questions below are designed to help you identify your goals for your relationship with your children and examine some of the obstacles you may have encountered along the way.

Fantasize for a moment. Imagine your children in 10 or 15 years, telling their friends, their partners or perhaps their own children about what a terrific parent you were. Regardless of the reality of your current situation, identify at least five ways you would like your children to complete the following sentence:

My mom/dad was great because . . .

1. _____

2. _____

3. _____

4. _____

5. _____

6. _____

In what ways are any of the above statements true at this time?

_____

_____

What do you want your relationship with your child to look like 10 or 15 years from now?

_____

_____

Most of us have been taught certain things about how parents and their children *should* act. Think of some of the messages you've received and complete the following sentences:

A parent should . . .   A teenager should . . .

1. _____   1. _____

   _____   _____

2. _____   2. _____

   _____   _____

3. _____   3. _____

   _____   _____

4. _____   4. _____

   _____   _____

5. _____   5. _____

   _____   _____

6. _____   6. _____

   _____   _____

7. _____   7. _____

   _____   _____

8. _____   8. _____

_____   _____

In what ways might these "shoulds" be interfering with your parenting goals?

_____

_____

_____

Imagine that the "Great Relationship Fairies" were coming to your house tonight while everyone was asleep. What would your family look like tomorrow?

_____

_____

_____

What are you willing to change in order to build the type of relationships you described in your answer to the last question?

_____

_____

_____

Is There Hope?

It is easier to start changing parenting behaviors when your children are young. And if you have young kids at home, the ideas in this book can certainly help you avoid some headaches down the road.

Under the best conditions, the teen years can be a trial for any parent. If kids haven't developed self-responsibility and self-management skills, the outcomes of their making poor choices at this point in their lives can be devastating.

Yet, I've seen some badly damaged relationships turn around. It's easier to build on a foundation of win-win and mutual respect for one another's needs for acceptance, space and power, but it is also possible to renegotiate a powering relationship in midstream.

It may be hard to start taking care of yourself in relationships in which, for whatever reasons, you've been a Doormat, and harder still, at least at first, to be taken seriously. But it is possible to take a stand and hold your ground even if you are shaky at first.

The point is, as you may have heard, nothing changes until something changes. If you're not happy with your

relationships with your kids (or anyone else for that matter), you've only got a few choices. On one hand, you can
complain, wait for them to change or try to control the
way they're acting. Chances are you've tried these tactics
at least a few times, probably without much success. On
the other hand, you can change the way you relate to and
respond to your kids. Certain parenting behaviors are
more likely to inspire positive outcomes than others, and
as we begin practicing these behaviors, the relationships
— and the responses of those around us — change.

As long as you're both alive, there is hope. But, for
better or for worse, change will start with you.

Eight

How Boundaries Work

Boundaries let the world know your limits: who you are, what you're comfortable or uncomfortable with and what you are willing to do, accept or take responsibility for. They let people know when, where or under what conditions you are available or willing to do something. Boundaries are primarily for taking care of yourself. They talk about you — what *you* need in this situation, what *you* are willing to tolerate — although they can offer a way for you to accommodate someone else's needs as well. Boundaries give people important information they can use in making decisions about how best to relate to you.

Boundaries are neither punitive nor intended to teach people lessons. They simply let people know what their choices are. We can look at a store's business hours as a kind of boundary. Let's say the store is open from 9:00 A.M. until 9:00 P.M. To make this work best for the owner, the employees and the customers, this information is made quite clear and is available to anyone who visits the store. The owner might post the hours on the door and include them in the ads, and would certainly make this information available to anyone who called. As a customer, you know or can find out whether this store is open *before* you drive there at midnight.

If the store respects its own boundaries and you get there after 9:00 P.M., it will probably be closed, no matter what your intention, regardless of what delayed you and in spite of what you thought the hours were.

The store is not closed to punish you for your delay or misunderstanding. It's not closed to teach you a lesson. It's not closed to mess with your mind. It's just closed. Period.

Without boundaries, our ways of taking care of ourselves are fairly limited and often destructive. We're more likely to take things personally, get hooked into power struggles and generate resentments. We may become intensely attached to being right, "winning" and getting satisfaction — goals that can take a rather hefty toll on relationships.

Since boundaries are positive, pro-active and mutually-respectful, they can help us avoid behaviors that hurt or alienate others. Boundaries allow for healthier relationships because they do not attack or judge someone else's behavior or criticize someone else's worth. For example, instead of telling a child that he is lazy and thoughtless because his lateness keeps everyone waiting, a boundary tells him that he needs to be ready to leave by a specific time if he plans to go along.

HELP PEOPLE BE RESPONSIBLE
FOR THEIR ACTIONS

Boundaries do not attempt to control or change anyone else. They do not suggest that someone should feel or act differently. Boundaries help people assume responsibility for their choices: if your child isn't ready, he doesn't get to go. This outcome is not a punishment for not doing what you wanted, it is the natural consequence of the choices he has made. He is still emotionally "safe" because in no way has his worth or dignity come under fire. He just wasn't ready on time. Of course you may all feel frustrated or disappointed, but you won't be held up — which was the real issue here — and he won't be rushed, nagged or put down.

Boundaries do not make someone else responsible for your feelings or actions. Instead of telling your daughter that you're feeling frustrated by the fact that she ties up the phone night after night, a boundary asks for a commitment to a plan that will accommodate your specific telephone needs. Rather than talking about how hurt and angry you feel when you find dishes all over the countertop as you're about to start dinner, you can announce, "I'll start dinner if the counters are cleaned by 5:30." You may need to fix yourself a sandwich and allow the rest of the family to do the same, but you won't have to cook and pre-clean too. More important, you've avoided blaming others for your feelings.

NO PUT-DOWNS . . .

Boundaries eliminate the need for put-downs, powering and sarcasm. When your kid tells you he wants to keep the car out until 4:00 A.M., you don't have to respond with, "What!? Are you crazy?" You can simply let him know, "That won't work for me." This boundary also leaves room for negotiating a time both of you can live with.

No anger, judgment or manipulation. No need to step on anyone's feelings or to feel you "gotta win this one." In fact, it's nothing personal at all.

How different from the way most of us have learned to have our needs met! This lack of experience with boundaries — both setting them and hearing them — can create the temptation to look for a specific way to structure a "boundary sentence." However, there is no particular formula or set of words for expressing a boundary. In fact, a boundary might even be a single word like, "No," "Stop" or "Enough." The point is mutual accommodation — taking care of yourself with regard for the other person — and thus, the structure of the statement itself is secondary. As we get better at recognizing and respecting our

own needs and limits, and recognizing and respecting other people's needs and limits, the boundaries will find expression in effective, nonhurtful ways.

So before we discuss the mechanics of expressing a
boundary, let's look at the type of parenting relationship in
which boundary-setting is a natural part. For most of us,
boundary setting requires certain behaviors that unfortunately are not a part of many parent-child relationships.

Part II is devoted to these behaviors, how they support
self-care in relationships and what they actually look,
sound and feel like when you are face-to-face with your
child.

PART II

TWENTY INGREDIENTS OF HEALTHY PARENT-CHILD RELATIONSHIPS

Nine

Introduction:
The Big Picture

In the following chapters, we'll examine the pieces of a healthy, loving relationship in which boundary-setting and boundary-respecting are natural parts of the way people relate to one another.

But first, a word of caution: It's easy to get hung up on short-range goals and conflicts that demand immediate attention and, therefore, to lose sight of the big picture. If you find yourself impatiently perusing the following chapters wondering, "Yeah, yeah. Love, respect, communicate, anticipate. Big deal. What's all this got to do with doing the dishes?" that's probably what's happening. Without minimizing the importance of chores, curfews or even basic issues such as trust, the conflicts we experience in our relationships simply may be indications of glitches in the bigger picture, namely, the quality of the relationship itself.

You may have noticed, probably with some frustration, that this book has not dealt much with "fixing" specific problems. It's not that taking out the trash, doing home-work or staying clean and sober isn't important. It's just that focusing on these goals instead of the relationship can be rather shortsighted. In the long run, it's simply more effective to build a positive context for dealing with problems rather than attacking specific problems them-selves, even though it undoubtedly will take longer. This may even appear to encourage you to be willing to tolerate unacceptable behavior. Not so. You've just shifted your emphasis from the problems to the relationship. When the negative patterns in the relationship begin to disap-pear, many problematic behaviors — especially those in-tended to gain power, attention, escape or revenge — are no longer necessary. Remember, we're talking about re-negotiating relationships, changing the way the relation-ships work. As that happens, many conflicts will take care of themselves.

Keep in mind that each of the following chapters de-scribes specific elements that work together to create the relationship. Ultimately, each element is necessary to pro-vide the kind of context in which positive interactions occur. If we attempt to incorporate one element of a healthy relationship in the absence of many others, it's not fair to expect much in terms of long-term overall change.

Certainly any change in the relationship is ultimately capable of changing the relationship itself. However, we will run into problems when we try to introduce a new parenting behavior completely out of context. For example, attempts to empower in the absence of trust are likely to fail. Expecting responsibility is a set-up for disaster in an environment in which blaming and helplessness prevail. And one stab at win-win in an otherwise win-lose context won't make much sense to anyone concerned.

Loving, mutually-respectful relationships require that the majority of the following behaviors be present most of the time. So watch the temptation to focus on individ-ual pieces of healthy relationships in isolation from one another.

To illustrate: Have you ever prepared a recipe and left out an ingredient? The end result might have looked okay, and may have even tasted okay, but you probably had greater success when you included everything the recipe called for. If you left out one or more of the basic ingredients, I suspect the outcome may have been somewhat disappointing. (You may have even sworn off cooking for a while.)

By themselves, each ingredient of a healthy, positive relationship is extremely important, as is each ingredient of a recipe. Most cookies, for example, call for some sort of flour and don't turn out very well without it. But as important as this ingredient is, you would hardly expect your cookies to be very tasty if you only use flour.

Likewise, it's unfair to expect satisfying relationships if you only have love. Granted, without love you won't get too far. But relationships take a lot more than love. Love is just one ingredient. You're far more likely to end up with the kind of relationship you want when you work to develop the entire relationship — the big picture — rather than just one piece of it.

As you read the next few chapters, watch for the things you're already doing "right." Look for ways to maximize and perhaps fine-tune whatever you've already got working for you.

If the next section sounds very different from the way things are currently working in your family, focus on "pieces" that are possible at the moment. The exercise at the end of each chapter will help you identify little things you can do to begin the process of change. Be careful not to get bogged down in the prospect of a complete relationship overhaul.

Even in the most complex recipe, when the ingredients are all working together, they've each been prepared and added individually, simmered and nurtured into a product that eventually goes beyond the sum of its parts.

Ten

Love

Let's start with the most basic ingredient — love. When creating an emotional environment that is conducive to setting boundaries, you don't get any more basic than this.

I haven't met many parents who didn't love their kids, although most will, at least occasionally, find their kids a bit bewildering, annoying or even unlikeable. The sad thing is that while most parents probably love their kids no matter what, many only demonstrate their love when their kids behave or look a certain way.

The challenge of unconditional love is not just showing it when your kids' grades are great, when their rooms are neat or when they bring the car back on time, but being able to show it when *none* of the above is true. If this sounds impossible, you may be confusing the idea of loving your children with loving how your children are acting.

This, then, is a great place to distinguish between a person's worth and his behavior. There will be times when you'll be tempted to reduce your kid to "someone who never cleans her room," but rest assured that is not who your child is. That is how she acts. At least for now.

Maybe forever. But even if this is her most consistent and enduring behavior, it's only one of many. It is neither who she is, nor a reflection of her worth as a human being. The good news is: While the behavior may not be lovable to you, your child still can be.

A relationship context for boundary-setting assumes that we're all basically lovable, worthwhile individuals who sometimes behave in not-so-lovable ways. In fact, the more effectively you can separate your child's behavior from her worth, the more easily you'll be able to love, accept and respect who she is.

This is especially important when conflicts arise. The ability to separate behavior from "being" allows you to attack problems without attacking people. In other words, you can deal with the outcome of your child's lateness, sloppiness or whatever, without making it a character issue. This leaves you free to love your children no matter what, and it leaves the children free to be lovable and acceptable regardless of the choices they make.

EXERCISE

List at least six ways you demonstrate love for your children.

1. _____

2. _____

3. _____

4. _____

5. _____

6. _____

7. _____

8. _____

9. _____

Which of the above behaviors have you demonstrated in the past 24 hours?

_____

_____

Which of the above behaviors have you demonstrated in the past week?

_____

_____

Which of the above behaviors do your children especially seem to appreciate?

_____

_____

What are some other ways your children might enjoy being shown love?

_____

_____

_____

Which of the above ways are you willing to incorporate into your repertoire of loving behaviors?

_____

_____

In the past, what has prevented you from demonstrating love for your children?

_____

_____

_____

Describe a time you were able to express unconditional love in spite of your child's behavior.

_____

_____

_____

Identify strategies you currently use — or might use in the future — to remind yourself that your children are not their behaviors.

_____

_____

_____

Identify two things you plan to do in the next 24 hours to demonstrate that you love your children no matter what else happens.

1. _____

2. _____

Eleven

Accept

At first glance, acceptance may seem very similar to love. Indeed, loving someone unconditionally means accepting who he is unconditionally. This is why it's so important to be able to separate people from behaviors. You will certainly have to deal with unacceptable behavior from time to time, but can you do so without making your children themselves unacceptable?

Being acceptable means that who you are is okay, just the way you are. It's hard to imagine feeling loved if you don't feel accepted. If you grew up with conditional love, you probably felt acceptable only when you looked or behaved a certain way. If you grew up with a great deal of criticism, shaming and disapproval, or with parents who felt threatened or uncomfortable with who you were, you probably didn't feel accepted at all.

UNCONDITIONAL ACCEPTANCE

It's easy to accept the things about your kids that you like and that reflect well on you. The challenge of acceptance is to be able to appreciate differences, let go of agendas and expectations and allow your children to become the people they are rather than the people you would like them to be. Again, this requires separating being — personality, preferences and proclivities — from behavior.

Acceptance means that your child can hate broccoli, the opera or even football, for example, no matter how important these things are to you. It means acknowledging that *your* dream of little Susie becoming a world-renown brain surgeon may be inconsistent with *her* dreams, aspirations or capabilities.

Acceptance frees you from going crazy when your son announces that he has decided to get his ear pierced. (In fact, one mother told me that her son was so disappointed that she didn't react to this news, he simply didn't bother having it done.) It allows you not to be embarrassed by your kids' appearance, their musical preferences or taste in friends. It helps you recognize that as separate, unique individuals, your children are not responsible for representing your values and inclinations.

Acceptance allows Type A parents to get along with Type B kids. It allows parents to be just as proud of the kid who doesn't make the team as the kid who does. And when specific behaviors are unacceptable, it allows you to deal with the behavior in ways that are far less damaging to your children — or to the relationship.

Unconditional acceptance frees children to discover for themselves who they really are by living with various experiences long enough to see how well their choices work for them. In fact, living in an environment of love and acceptance often makes it unnecessary for kids to pull some of the bonehead stunts they might pull just to assert their power and independence. Plus, with this kind of support, when kids do make dumb choices, they tend to notice sooner and are better able to change their course before things get too bad.

EXERCISE

Identify five things you have in common with each of your children (use additional paper for additional children or for other adults to complete). You might consider traits such as appearance, interests, aspirations or personality characteristics.

Child _____   Child _____

1. _____   1. _____

2. _____   2. _____

3. _____   3. _____

4. _____   4. _____

5. _____   5. _____

Child _____   Child _____

1. _____   1. _____

2. _____   2. _____

3. _____   3. _____

4. _____   4. _____

5. _____   5. _____

Which of the above characteristics do you value the most?

_____

_____

_____

Why are these commonalities important to you?

_____

_____

_____

Which of the above characteristics concern (or annoy) you the most?

_____

_____

_____

What bothers you about these commonalities?

_____

_____

_____

Identify five ways in which you differ from each of your children (use additional paper for additional children or for other adults to complete):

Child _____   Child _____

1. _____   1. _____

2. _____   2. _____

3. _____   3. _____

4. _____   4. _____

5. _____   5. _____

Child _____   Child _____

1. _____   1. _____

2. _____   2. _____

3. _____   3. _____

4. _____   4. _____

5. _____   5. _____

Which of the above differences concern (or annoy) you the most?

_____

_____

_____

What bothers you about these differences?

_____

_____

_____

Which of the above differences do you appreciate the most?

_____

_____

_____

For what reasons do you appreciate these differences?

_____

_____

_____

Which items in your lists have been the easiest for you to accept?

_____

_____

_____

In what ways has your acceptance enhanced your relationship with your children?

_____

_____

_____

Which characteristics have been the most difficult for you to accept?

_____

_____

_____

In what ways has this difficulty presented obstacles to a good relationship with your children?

_____

_____

_____

Given the possibility that what you find difficult to accept about your children may not change, in what ways might you be willing to change in order to find your children more acceptable?

_____

_____

_____

Identify two things you plan to do in the next 24 hours to demonstrate that you accept your children no matter what else happens.

1. _____

2. _____

Twelve

Separate

Healthy relationships are made up of separate, complete individuals who are able to need and depend on one another in healthy ways and still feel okay about themselves, regardless of the other person's interests, values or behaviors. This is perhaps the greatest challenge for any parent: being able to acknowledge his or her child's separateness. Yet the ability to separate — and *be* separate — is essential to being able to love and accept the other person unconditionally. That ability also is essential to being able to take care of oneself, especially when the other person is behaving in unlovable or unacceptable ways.

This challenge will be especially difficult for the parent who grew up with the message that her value depended on someone else's approval, which depended on her ability to meet that person's expectations. Are your children vulnerable, for example, to your concerns with what the neighbors, or perhaps your in-laws, will think? Do you push your children to meet someone else's standards simply to avoid conflict or disapproval of your parenting?

To what degree does your sense of success, serenity and self-esteem hinge on the choices your children make? If you see your children as reflections of yourself and your worth, you may find it hard to accept their uniqueness. If you believe that your children are responsible for "making you look good," they probably *won't* have the emotional security to take risks, try new things or make mistakes.

Plus, think of the stress that parental enmeshment can place on the relationship. If *you* feel like a failure when their grades drop, when they wear torn blue jeans or when they get in trouble at school, you're going to feel constant pressure to make your children be a certain way in order to feel okay about yourself. This won't leave much space for acceptance. Instead you create the potential for conflicts, power struggles, frustration and disappointments. And you set yourself up as an easy target for an angry kid who wants power or revenge.

Unconditional love and acceptance require separation — the ability to separate who your children are from how they act, as well as the ability to separate who they are from who you are. Messages, whether direct or indirect, that suggest the parent's happiness, and sense of competence, are tied to the child's choices put a tremendous amount of pressure on the child to caretake the parent's needs. When the parent's agenda is very different from the child's, the child may comply for the parent's approval or rebel to assert his independence. Either way, the focus is on the parent's needs and often the child's sense of who he is gets lost along the way.

If ever you're going to run into difficulty accepting who your child is becoming, chances are it will be during the adolescent and teen years when changes occur fast and furious. If you often feel as if your kid is letting you down, now might be a good time to look at your own expectations and your attachment to him "turning out" a certain way.

NOT INDIFFERENCE OR ABANDONMENT

Separateness does not mean indifference or abandonment. It simply means that you are not your children and they are not you. There is great freedom in this for all concerned. Separateness allows you to hold them accountable for their behavior. You don't have to bail them out or fix their mistakes. You don't have to take aspirin when they get headaches. You can let them have a bad day or be in a grumpy mood (although you may want to keep your distance on those occasions). Your sense of worth is not dependent on events over which you may have only limited influence. You can become an agent of facilitation and guidance, rather than one of control or manipulation.

Your children can explore who they are and become who they were meant to be. They don't need to self-abandon or people-please for approval because their sense of approval comes from the unconditional love and acceptance they get for being themselves.

EXERCISE

When you were a child, was your behavior, achievements, values or appearance tied to your parents' sense of esteem and success? If so, how?

_____

_____

How did your parents communicate this to you?

_____

_____

How did you respond to this attitude?

_____

_____

Are the behavior, achievement, values or appearance of
your children tied to your own sense of esteem and success? If so, how?

_____

_____

How have you communicated this to your children?

_____

_____

How have your children responded to this?

_____

_____

In what areas in your relationship with your children
are you able to feel most separate?

_____

_____

In what areas in your relationship with your children
do you feel the least separate (most enmeshed)?

_____

_____

How has this affected your relationship with your children?

_____

_____

Identify one issue over which you are willing to become
more separate from your children.

_____

_____

Thirteen

Respect

I'll bet you can think of a dozen reasons why you deserve your children's respect. Respect is an essential part of an adult-child relationship. Few parents would argue that. However, at least a few of us still see respect as a one-way street, something kids owe parents. But in healthy, loving families respect goes both ways. So, given that you want and deserve respect from your kids, are you willing to give it back?

If you love your child unconditionally and are able to accept who she is, regardless of how she acts or looks, this part probably won't be too much of a challenge. You've already got a good sense of your child's worth as a human being and recognize that, as such, she is worthy of respect. If your parents treated you respectfully when you were a child, you're even further ahead of the game.

Yet the idea of mutual respect between parents and children can be frightening to parents when it implies a loss of power or control. Rest assured that mutual respect in parent-child relationships does not undermine parental authority. In fact, quite the opposite is true. While treating people respectfully doesn't guarantee cooperative behavior, it does contribute to an atmosphere in which agreements and commitments can be reached more quickly and effectively.

Many authoritarian parents operate with the idea that simply being the parent entitles them to respect. Many believe that respect will come to them as the result of strictness, rules and, when all else fails, simply demanding it. This is, after all, how many of their adult role models behaved. Unfortunately these parents confuse respect with fear — one doesn't legislate respect with rules and commands.

Indeed, treating someone disrespectfully might appear to give you power in the short run. You might get your way. But consider the long-term effects such interaction can have on you, the child and the relationship.

I get nervous when I hear parents say things like, "I don't care if my kid likes me, as long as he respects me." My concerns are about the likelihood of children genuinely respecting someone they dislike. Most likely these kids are just watching their backs and acting in a way that appears respectful simply to stay safe.

Respect for your children means accepting that they have the right to their dignity. They have the right to affect their lives by making choices that don't hurt others. They have the right to privacy about their bodies and personal space, the right to their feelings and opinions, the right to make mistakes and learn from these experiences. Just like you.

In terms of everyday interactions, this may mean that you knock on one another's doors when they are shut. It may mean not interfering in one another's choice of clothing or hairstyles. It may mean not going through one another's closets or drawers without permission.

Respect may mean resisting the urge to speak to your child in ways that you would consider rude or disrespectful if someone — especially your child — spoke to you that way. It may mean learning to say "please" and "thank you."

It may mean respecting your child's resiliency enough to say no, to maintain your own boundaries or to confront problems directly. It may mean having enough respect for their intelligence to stop solving problems for them or telling them what to do. It may mean respecting their need for control in their lives by asking for input before making a decision that will affect them.

It may mean not making a big deal about something you'd never comment on if your child were another adult. (I once overheard two parents lecture and shame their kids for putting ketchup on their french fries the wrong way. I'd bet my last dime these parents would never do that to you or me.)

However it translates in your family and relationships, respect is the foundation of doing unto others as we would have others do unto us. And far more important, it is the foundation for long-term loving relationships.

EXERCISE

In what ways do you demonstrate respect for your children's interests and preferences?

_____

_____

In what ways do you respect their need for privacy and space?

_____

_____

In what ways do you show respect for your children's feelings and opinions?

_____

_____

How do you show your children that you respect their ability to solve their own problems?

_____

_____

In what other ways do you show respect for your children?

_____

_____

In what ways do your children demonstrate respect for you?

_____

_____

Why do you suppose your children behave respectfully when they do? What have you done to inspire this behavior?

_____

_____

If their respectful behavior is predominantly motivated by a fear of your anger or disapproval, what might you do differently to assure their emotional safety and still generate respect?

_____

_____

If your children have not behaved very respectfully lately, what types of behaviors would you like to start seeing? Be specific.

_____

_____

How consistently do *you* demonstrate the behaviors you've just described? Be specific.

_____

_____

Which of the above behaviors are you willing to start — or continue — exhibiting in your relationship with your children?

_____

_____

What else might you do (or change) to inspire your children to treat you respectfully?

_____

_____

Identify two things you plan to do in the next 24 hours to demonstrate that you respect your children no matter what else happens.

1. _____

2. _____

Fourteen

Anticipate

Many of the conflicts that arise in relationships can be avoided by anticipating what you're going to need in various situations, anticipating what your kids are likely to need and anticipating, as much as possible, how they're likely to respond. Anticipation is the better part of *pro-acting*, allowing you to set a boundary *before* a conflict occurs. Anticipation is about prevention. It is the healthy alternative to *re-acting*, which forces us to look for ways to deal with the kid after he's blown it.

Sometimes anticipation simply involves a little forethought and common sense. You need to return a phone call by eight o'clock? Don't wait until 7:55 to blow up at your kids for tying up the phone all night. Let them know earlier in the day and request a commitment ahead of time to have the phone free when you'll need it.

You want to spend some time with your kids? Avoid competing with time they've committed to friends, hobbies or their favorite TV show. Plan for a time that's free and convenient for everyone.

You want liver for dinner and your kids don't "do" liver? Why force the issue? Make enough liver for yourself (and any other liver-lovers in the family), and let the others make sandwiches, reheat leftovers or send out for pizza.

To some extent, you can predict certain behaviors based on past experiences. You've probably lived with your kids long enough to know that they are used to being called to the table several times, that they still don't know what the laundry hamper is for and that they will always want extra money before the end of the week. Now you can either use this information to be grouchy and self-righteous, which probably won't get you what you want, or to make a plan that will work in everyone's favor.

In anticipating, ask yourself, "How many times am I willing to call my kids to the table?" "Am I willing to wash the clothes *and* play hide-and-seek with them?" "How much money am I comfortable giving the kids each week and what options can I offer them for earning or borrowing for special occasions?" Then set your boundaries accordingly.

Perhaps your kids have learned that they can get out of chores, responsibilities or curfews by being loud, rude and defiant. But what would happen if those tactics no longer worked for them, neither causing you to react nor cave in? It might help you to identify the times and circumstances under which the greatest conflicts are likely to occur. What are your kids trying to accomplish here? What do they need? How can you meet some of these needs in nondisruptive ways to reduce their need to act out? What would they rather be doing? Perhaps connecting what you want with what they want will make cooperation more likely.

And what about you? There will be times when you will naturally slide dangerously close to the edge, particularly if you haven't set a boundary ahead of time (and even more particularly if you have and it's been ignored). Can you think of a way to disengage before you do or say something hurtful or before you allow yourself to be violated in any way?

Sometimes boundaries will have to shift to accommodate certain situations. While the stereo may not bother you normally, can you anticipate that it might when you have a headache, are entertaining company or you're taking a call from your boss? These occasions call for boundaries you won't need to use every day. Anticipating, even from moment to moment when necessary, lets you express a need before you're tempted to throw the stereo — and the kid — through the nearest window.

Think situations through *before* you end up in the middle of something that needs to be defused. If you're headed to the mall and don't want to spend the entire day there, maybe today isn't the day to take the kids. Or maybe you'll avoid a conflict or two by offering a ride to the mall only to those kids who agree, ahead of time, to be ready to leave when you are, or who are willing to take the bus home by a certain time. If you're going to a relative's home for a few days and you know your kids are going to be bored there, suggest they take a friend along, pack a few videos to watch (or books to read) or maybe even stay home.

You can't anticipate everything that might come up. There are probably more than a few parents who have wondered why they never thought to tell Junior not to hang from the drapes, flood the bathroom or cook marshmallows in the toaster. But the more you can anticipate the things your kids are going to want to do, watch, buy, get, play with or have, the better you can plan your own parenting behaviors. And that will create an environment in which everyone's needs and wants are considered.

EXERCISE

In the past, at what times, under what circumstances or about which issues have most of your conflicts with your children occurred?

_____

_____

Identify several areas of conflict you anticipate may arise in the near future. For each potential conflict, identify what you will probably need in that situation. Then describe what your children will probably need in that situation.

Area of Conflict	My Needs	My Children's Needs
1. _____	_____	_____
2. _____	_____	_____
3. _____	_____	_____
4. _____	_____	_____
5. _____	_____	_____
6. _____	_____	_____
7. _____	_____	_____
8. _____	_____	_____

Communicate

Have you ever been tripped up by an assumption? You had what seemed to be a perfectly reasonable picture of how things were supposed to be, then found the reality to be quite different.

Part of the reason we go to all the trouble of anticipating our needs is to let others know what they are. Yet there is a well-established tradition in many families that discourages or even shames us for asking for what we need. Many of us are conditioned *not* to communicate our boundaries. We switch to less effective behaviors like wishing, assuming and expecting because those behaviors seem a little safer. (When you consider that these behaviors let us be victims of other people's choices and allow us to be "right" at their expense, you can see how difficult it is to give them up.)

UNSPOKEN BOUNDARIES

If you've heard yourself say things like "I shouldn't have to tell you that" or "You should have known," you have probably experienced a great deal of frustration and disappointment that might have been avoided if you had gone to the trouble of letting that person know what you wanted. Because even if you're right — if they indeed *should* have known — being right won't get you nearly the same positive results as communicating. (And it never feels quite as good as knowing you've taken care of yourself by expressing your needs.) Even when we do let people know what we want, we're still not assured of commitment or cooperation on their part. But how much less likely are we to be accommodated when we depend on the people around us to read our minds, operate with our priorities or even remember from "last time."

Part of the responsibility of having our boundaries respected involves making them known. If you don't want people to smoke in your house, it would be wiser to let them know before they light up, or even before they come over, than it would to hope they get the hint from your coughing spells and your attempts to fan their smoke away with a copy of the Surgeon General's report!

Communicating your wishes in the form of a boundary eliminates the need for pleas or threats. If you're going to need the phone at a specific time, let the family know: "I have an important conference call coming in at 7:30 tonight. You're welcome to use the phone as long as you're off by 7:15." If you've had win-win arrangements in place for a while, your kids are probably fairly cooperative because they know they can respect your boundaries and still have their needs met. In this case, you may not have to say anything else.

However, if you anticipate that your kids are going to depend on you to "get" them off the phone — which they probably will until they become more self-managing — it may be necessary to add other boundaries: "I'll let you know when it's ten after so you can wrap up your call in time." If you won't be able to remind them to get off the phone, you might even add: "I'll be tied up with paperwork until my call comes in, so you're responsible for getting off the phone in time. Did you plan to use the phone tonight? How do you intend to make sure it's free by 7:15?"

ANTICIPATE AND EXPRESS

Statements like "You guys can decide on v
tonight as long as you pick a place that has a salad bar" or
"I've had a rotten day. I need a half-hour to myself with
no noise and no interruptions" can anticipate and express
your needs in these specific situations. They can also give
your kids important information to use in meeting their
own needs without creating conflict for you. Whether it's
picking a restaurant they like or turning the TV up (or
even talking to you in 30 minutes), these are the payoffs
for cooperation. Knowing this up front makes cooperation
more likely.

BE SPECIFIC

In the process of letting people know what you want,
some techniques work better than others. For example,
specificity and clarity will help. Since telling your kids to
keep the music at a "reasonable volume" will probably have
a different meaning to them than it does to you, try something like "whatever volume I won't be able to hear in the
den" or "with the knob set on the number seven or below."

If your kids are typical of others their age, their idea of
"late," "good" or "clean" is probably a little different from
yours, too. Make sure your limits are clear, specific and
understandable to all concerned. What do you mean by
"a *decent* hour," "*behaving* at Aunt Martha's" or "putting
your things *away*"? If your kids' idea of a clean room
means that they can find most of the furniture in it, you
might all experience greater success if you specify what
"clean" means to you.

It can be helpful to communicate in writing. It's hard
to forget one's promise to take out the trash when one
finds a big reminder taped to the refrigerator or TV.
This is especially important if your kids remember better
by seeing than they do by hearing. For these children,
one sign that says that laundry "happens" at 9:00 A.M. on
Saturday may be infinitely more effective than a dozen
verbal reminders.

Sometimes conflicts occur because children simply don't know how to do a particular task or use a particular piece of equipment. Perhaps you can remember some disaster that involved putting too much soap in the washing machine, setting the oven too high or forgetting to put the lid on the blender. How many kids intuitively know how to use household appliances, manage their time or organize their "stuff"? Before simply demanding that your kids do something, consider whether or not they have the information, skills and developmental readiness they'll need.

You can increase the likelihood of cooperation and commitment by making it easier for your kids to succeed. This may mean taking the time to show them — sometimes more than once. Or writing down instructions in a language they can understand. It may mean using their mistakes as opportunities to help them refine their skills.

Communication that simply expresses limits, preferences and needs is far more effective than demands, threats, begging or shame. In addition, you can always sweeten the deal when your communication offers to accommodate *their* needs in the process, whether that need is to listen to music, have the car again next weekend or have clean clothes on Monday morning.

EXERCISE

When you want something from your kids, how do you let them know?

_____

_____

To what degree do these communication techniques inspire your children's cooperation?

_____

_____

If these techniques are working, why do you suppose they are?

_____

_____

If these techniques are not working, what might you do differently?

_____

_____

In what ways do these communication techniques enhance your relationships?

_____

_____

In what ways do these techniques create conflict in your relationships?

_____

_____

How might you avoid these conflicts in the future?

_____

_____

Empower

One of the most basic human needs is a need for power in one's life. You want it. I want it. And from about age two, your kids want it. I'm talking about believing that we can affect our environment and shape our own destinies, make choices and experience the outcomes and change what isn't working in our lives. A sense of personal power is absolutely essential to a person's ability to function responsibly and independently. It is the first line of defense against feeling helpless and victimized, and it is a key component of self-esteem. Empowerment is necessary for boundary-setting and other self-caring behaviors, such as just saying no.

The kind of personal power we need to foster in our children isn't power over others, power to hurt or power to disempower. It is the power of responsibility and self-management. In a global sense, empowerment means having the perception that *you can* make a difference.

This is exactly what we want for our kids, isn't it?

Then why does the idea of empowering kids — allowing and encouraging them to experience their own sense of power — make most parents' hair stand on end?

CHILDHOOD ISSUES

For one thing, there are your own personal history and childhood issues. If you grew up in a family in which your parents had all the power, if you spent much of your time on the losing end of a win-lose power relationship, the idea of your kids having power may be a little hard to accept. In fact, the more you depend on power over others to get results or feel successful, the more threatening the idea of empowering your children will seem. There may even be a certain seductiveness in the power of being a parent. (This is, after all, your chance to "win.")

In the same way, if your parents weren't around much or if, for some reason, they did not manage their responsibilities well, it may be hard to see how power can be shared in healthy ways.

Not surprisingly, most of us take an all-or-nothing approach to this issue. Whether our parents were threatened by, intimidated by or indifferent toward our need for power, very few of us have had models for empowering kids. Thus, we tend to deal with this issue by extremes. We worry that giving kids power will eliminate our own. In our fear of losing control, we resort to the most familiar technique for maintaining our power: disempowering the other person. We do this either by overcontrolling, undermining their attempts at independence or violating their dignity and sense of competence. When this makes us feel guilty, we overcompensate by going the other way, overindulging and not setting limits where they're needed. This in turn creates resentments which will come in handy when we need to rationalize our next attempts at disempowerment. Crazy, huh?

MIDDLE GROUND

Fortunately there is a middle ground. It may be reassuring to know that empowering your kids does *not* mean disempowering yourself. In a responsible parent-child relationship, the parent is still in charge in terms of setting limits and deciding what is and is not negotiable. The goal here — and the alternative to traditional win-lose dynamics — is establishing an environment in which your need for power does not require stripping anyone else of theirs. This environment is called "win-win" because it considers and attempts to accommodate the needs of all persons involved.

You may not be able to meet everyone's needs every time, but there are lots of ways to empower children and establish win-win in your family. First of all, you can create a sense of power for your children by offering them the opportunity to be heard. People feel valued when they know that their input is requested and seriously considered in the outcome of a decision that affects them. (Think of a time this happened to you. Even if you didn't get exactly what you wanted, I suspect your participation in the process made the outcome easier to accept.) As a parent, being able to just listen — hearing and respecting your child's opinions, priorities and desires — is an important aspect of empowerment.

You can also empower by offering your children choices about things that matter. You can give them the opportunity to make mistakes, self-correct and do things over until they get them right. You can provide them with opportunities to self-manage. Each of these experiences strengthens your children's perception that they can influence the course of their lives, which is, in the truest sense, what empowerment is all about.

EXERCISE

In what ways did your parents empower you?

_____

_____

How have these experiences influenced your parenting behaviors and attitudes?

_____

_____

In what ways did your parents disempower you?

_____

_____

How have these experiences influenced your parenting behaviors and attitudes?

_____

_____

In what ways have you allowed and encouraged your children to experience power in their lives?

_____

_____

What was their reaction when you encouraged power in your children's lives?

_____

_____

In what ways have you prevented or discouraged your children from experiencing power in their lives?

_____

_____

What was their reaction when you prevented or discouraged power in their lives?

_____

_____

What are you willing to do or change to help your children develop a sense of empowerment?

_____

_____

Accommodate

Let's face it. Kids have lots of needs. So do parents. And sometimes these needs clash. Conflicts between kids' and parents' needs can place a great deal of stress on the relationship, especially since traditional methods for resolving these conflicts can add considerably to this stress. Most families deal with conflicts in one win-lose form or another. In a powering relationship, the focus is almost exclusively on the needs of the parents. In a permissive relationship, the focus is almost exclusively on the needs of the children.

In either of these configurations, where one set of needs is met at the expense of the other, the relationship becomes unbalanced. After a while, the "losing" side is going to want to win and may act out in ways that will create even more stress. The alternative is a healthy, win-win relationship that strives to reduce relationship stress through mutual accommodation: "How can we both get what we want?"

Not all conflicts lend themselves to perfect win-win solutions, but the mere *attempt* to accommodate everyone's needs and preferences — or at least hear and consider them — can eliminate a great number of conflicts. People tend to be far more committed and cooperative in a group in which they feel valued, included and taken seriously.

There are potentially tremendous payoffs when parents can accommodate their children's needs without hurting themselves in the process — needs for belonging, success, space, recognition, safety, power and fun, for example. During adolescence, these needs can be so overwhelmingly strong, that kids will sometimes go to extremes to have them met. (For example, look at how many of these needs can be met by joining a gang. If a child isn't experiencing these things in the relatively safe confines of the family or even at school, it's easy to see the attraction the streets can hold.) Kids who have their needs met in healthy, constructive ways may be less inclined to numb themselves with substances or compulsive behavior than kids who don't. Also, kids who have their needs met generally don't have to people-please, although they tend to be fairly cooperative and are usually not too difficult to live with.

IMPLEMENTATION

I suspect that there's already a place in your value system that respects the fact that your kids have these needs. The question then becomes one of implementation. Actually there are lots of things you can do that will accommodate your kids' needs at little or no cost to your authority, self-esteem or peace of mind.

For example, offering choices accommodates power needs. Kids are less likely to resist chores they've been allowed to choose than chores they've been assigned. They're more likely to participate in activities in which they've had a say. They're more likely to respect curfews or telephone limits when they've been involved in setting them. They're more likely to enjoy meals when their vote is considered in the menu plan. In fact, the whole idea of having a choice is in itself quite empowering.

However, offering choices requires a bit of forethought and skill, and the best offers include some boundaries on your part. Let's say you're planning a family vacation and want some feedback from your kids before making the final decision. If you're open to simply brainstorming for a variety of ideas, you might start off with a general question like, "Where would you like to go for vacation?" and see what they have to say.

If your children have any understanding of geographical distances and a sense of what travel, food, lodging and entertainment expenses can run, you might want to be more specific about the amount of time you'll have, your budgetary constraints or which continent you have in mind. Unless none of these are actual concerns for you, these are the boundaries within which decisions will be made.

If your kids do not have much experience making decisions, you might want to offer two or three specific choices, any of which would work within your schedule and budget, rather than leaving the field wide open. Share the brochures, give everyone a chance to think about their options and take a vote.

Teenagers are frequently in the unfortunate position of having grown up with nearly every adult in their lives thinking and deciding for them, and yet being expected to be able to make decisions responsibly once they hit a certain age. While there are probably a few teenagers who could do everything from researching the activities available at various vacation spots to ordering special airline meals for everyone in the family, others would have a hard time deciding between the mountains or the beach. We need to challenge, not overwhelm.

BEGIN SMALL

If your child hasn't had much chance to exercise his decision-making muscles, start small and definitely with specific choices. (Although in many situations, you can certainly be open to other suggestions he might offer.)

For example, rather than asking each kid to plan a week's dinner menu, ask for ideas for specific meals. Rather than asking everyone to tell you how they plan to contribute to the annual spring cleaning, make a list of what needs to be done and ask everyone to identify three chores they're willing to do by a certain date.

Involvement promotes empowerment and a sense of belonging, too, especially as kids begin seeing how their ideas, suggestions and choices contribute to the results. Even when you can't accommodate specific requests, your ability to listen and appreciate their input will help tremendously. Trust issues that reflect a kid's need to feel safe are at stake here. A psychologically and emotionally safe environment allows children to share their ideas without exposing themselves to judgment or ridicule, no matter how impossible, unrealistic or off-the-wall their suggestions may be.

SAFETY FIRST

Safety allows for ideas that won't work. You can still validate your teens' wishes and clarify boundaries without putting down their ideas: "That's about a three-day drive from here. It would definitely be a fun place to visit when we have more than a week off" or "I'd love for the four of us to go to Hawaii, but I don't think $1,200 is going to do it for a trip like that." Safety also demands that you avoid offering choices you don't intend to honor, or choices that don't exist because you've actually already made the decision.

Safety can also be encouraged by making sure that all the options you offer your kids are acceptable to you. In other words, don't ask if they'd rather clean the kitchen or play video games in the hopes that they'll people-please by making the "right" choice. Avoid choices that are loaded with your approval or disapproval. Offer choices like "wash or dry," "rake the leaves or fold the laundry," or "any two chores on the list." And don't offer options that really aren't

options, like, "Do you want to run the vacuum?" unless
"no" is an acceptable answer.

Safety might mean understanding how to do a particular task, but it can also mean *not* understanding and being
able to ask for instruction, practice or help. It means that
your kids can fail without becoming failures. It means
being recognized for effort and persistence. It means having a chance to try again.

SUCCESS NEEDS

Closely connected to safety is the need for success.
Success happens best when kids are developmentally and
experientially ready for what the situation requires, when
the hurdles are possible to clear and when the demands
being placed on your kids push them to grow and perform
without those demands being unrealistic, overwhelming
or punitive.

Then there's the need for space. This may mean actual
physical space, like her own room or, if that's not possible,
a few drawers or a closet that is exclusively hers. It may
mean space in the course of a day — free time — to relax,
talk with friends, play and have fun or just do nothing. It
may mean emotional space to have her feelings and moods
without having to stuff them, deny them or defend them.

Accommodation requires awareness of your needs and
of theirs. It may require a shift in your thinking. It will
probably require some practice. But what better way to
build your relationship and communicate love, acceptance
and respect in the process?

EXERCISE

How have you been able to recognize and accommodate your children's needs for emotional and psychological
safety?

_____

_____

How have you recognized and accommodated their needs for belonging and inclusion?

_____

_____

How have you recognized and accommodated your children's needs for power and freedom?

_____

_____

How have you recognized and accommodated their need for success?

_____

_____

How have you recognized and accommodated their need for recognition?

_____

_____

How have you accomodated their need for fun?

_____

_____

How have you recognized and accommodated their needs for physical space and privacy?

_____

_____

How have you recognized and accommodated their need for emotional space?

_____

_____

In what other ways do your recognize and accommo-date your children's needs?

_____

_____

What else might you do to recognize and accommo-date your children's needs for emotional and psycholog-ical safety?

_____

_____

What else could you do that would recognize and ac-commodate your children's needs for belonging and inclu-sion?

_____

_____

What other actions would acknowledge and accommo-date your children's needs for power and freedom?

_____

_____

What else could you do to recognize and accommodate your children's need for success?

_____

_____

In what other ways could you acknowledge and accom-modate your children's need for recognition?

_____

_____

What else could you do to accommodate your children's need for fun?

_____

_____

In what other ways could you acknowledge and accommodate your children's needs for physical space and
privacy?

_____

_____

What else could you do to recognize and accommodate
your children's need for emotional space?

_____

_____

In what other ways could you recognize and accommodate your children's needs?

_____

_____

Eighteen

Motivate

In healthy, functional family groups, individuals contribute to a peaceful and cooperative co-existence. Part of this contribution comes in the forms of unconditional love and acceptance, mutual respect, and honest and direct communication. But there's another level of contribution that invites participation from every family member, and that's the division of labor: the idea of everyone doing his or her part and everyone pitching in.

Even in the healthiest families, a common source of conflict is a lack of teamwork. By the time kids hit adolescence, most are developmentally capable of doing a majority of the chores or running most of the appliances required for routine household maintenance. Yet how many awaken each day in joyful anticipation of another opportunity to do these things?

If your child requires no more motivation than the thrill of a newly-vacuumed carpet, you might want to skip this chapter. If, on the other hand, your kids would rather step over three-foot-high piles of towels in the bathroom than hang them up, it'll probably be worthwhile to look at how motivation works.

CHOICES AND THE MOMENT

Actually, it's pretty simple. In fact, when it comes to motivating people — that is, getting them to do things they wouldn't ordinarily do — there are really only two points any of us need to know. One: In every situation, we always have choices. Even in do-it-or-else situations, we always have a choice. And two: We always make the choice that appears to be the most need-fulfilling at that moment. In other words, we do what pays off the best for us, or what we think will pay off the best for us.

All choices have a payoff — a consequence or outcome — and it is the probable payoff, or sometimes the avoidance of a particular payoff, that makes motivation work. Perhaps you made your bed this morning because you like getting into a made bed at night. Or because you wanted a place to put the clean laundry while you were putting it away. Maybe you wanted to please another family member who really values made beds or to avoid negative comments from the person who is coming over to visit this afternoon. Maybe you like the way the room looks when the bed is made, or find that making the bed helps you to be less of a slob about the rest of the room. Perhaps you just don't feel "done" until your bed is made — it's just something you do every day.

If none of these things is important to you, you may not have bothered making your bed today. Having the free time, the comfort of a "lived-in" decor or the freedom and power to refuse to do a chore you see as pointless paid off better for you.

Even "negative" choices pay off for us. Staying up way past our bedtime allows us to finish a book we can't put down. Continuing to smoke allows us to avoid the pain of withdrawal. Staying in a relationship with a controlling partner allows us to avoid taking responsibility for our own lives (and gives us something to complain about, too). Not sticking up for ourselves allows us to avoid someone else's anger or the possibility of them leaving us. Bailing our kids out time and time again allows us to feel important and necessary, and perhaps lets us live up to somebody's idea of being a good parent.

LOOKING AT THE MOTIVE

So it is with kids. In fact, you might find it interesting to look at your children from time to time and ask yourself, "What is he getting out of resisting this activity? What's in it for him to do what I ask?"

There are several good reasons for examining your kids' motives. For one thing, it can help you identify some effective ways to motivate them, if they're especially resistant, by connecting what you want with what they want. Chances are you've been doing this in one way or another all along. In some circles, this is called *contingency management*: making something desirable — the payoff — contingent on something else that is usually less desirable.

If your kids wash the car because they just love washing cars, you don't really need to motivate them. The payoff, which in this case is the pleasure of washing the car, is built in. But what if they don't particularly love car washing, yet the completion of this chore is part of the agreement for getting to use the car this weekend? You might find them much more willing to do this chore, but only if getting the car is more need-fulfilling than *not* washing it.

ANGER OR APPROVAL AS MOTIVATOR

Another thing to watch for is a tendency to use anger or approval as a motivator. How often do your kids cooperate simply to stay on your good side? How often do you depend on an angry reaction, whether it manifests as an insult, a lecture, a tirade or disapproval, shaming or physical violence, to get you what you want? Is conditional love and acceptance the force behind your children's cooperative behavior? This is the way most families operate, using some form of do-it-or-else, with "else" implying "I will hurt you in some way." This is what many of us know best.

So what's the problem? It's simple: anger and approval depend on people-pleasing and caretaking in order to work. Your children will have to find the need for your approval, or the fear of your anger, more pressing than whatever they get out of not doing what you want. This strategy is often ineffective with teens, who may opt for power, revenge or peer approval instead. And when it does work, think of the cost! Using anger or approval to get what you want from people communicates, "You are safe and worthwhile as long as you do what I want." If these are the motivators you rely on, you are essentially offering your kids a choice between caretaking and rebellion. Some choice, huh?

Remove The Reaction

The alternative is eliminating your reaction from the equation, which means looking for something else that will pay off for the kid. She takes the trash out, for example, so her room won't smell or so she can resume phone privileges when her chores are done — *not* so that Mom and Dad won't get mad at her. The idea is to connect some meaningful, positive outcome to what you're asking — an outcome that has nothing to do with how you are going to feel or act.

If your kids are not cooperating with a request or a boundary, asking yourself how this resistance is paying off for them can lead you to some more positive alternatives. In some cases it's power. Is refusing to cooperate a way to "win" or get attention in your family? If so, offering input or choices about the situation in question can defuse some of that conflict, as can accommodating power needs in constructive ways to other areas of their lives.

If the resistance comes from the kids' inability to see any meaning or purpose in doing something they don't like doing, you can reduce resistance by attaching some meaning to it. Putting clothes in the hamper or learning how to do the laundry means you have clean clothes next week. Making sure your friends go outside to smoke means that they are welcome to return. Finishing homework or chores means you have access to the TV or video games. Putting the power tools back means you can use them again next time you need them.

Unfortunately, some kids have to go a week or two without clean clothes, not be able to have certain people over for a while, miss a few TV shows or borrow tools from someone else before they actually understand that there are rewards for making certain choices. In fact, you're going to *want* them to blow it from time to time because this is a great way for them to learn how they can influence the quality of their lives one way or the other. This is what responsibility is about: seeing the connection between what we do and what happens when we make those choices.

Don't Fight About Everything

As a word of caution, pick your fights carefully. One of the best ways to reduce conflict in the household is to reduce the number of things you're trying to control. For example, if your kid's room looks like a war zone, you might indeed be able to find lots of ways to motivate him to clean it. Or you can take the best advice I've ever heard on this issue: check for bugs and shut the door. Some parents attach contingencies that require no food in the room or an occasional change of linens and leave it at that. Some kids can get along fine in a room that would make another person crazy. As long as the chaos is confined to his side of the door, it doesn't have to affect your life at all. If it gets to be too much for him, he can always change what isn't working. This is how we learn self-management, which happens a lot faster when someone isn't busy managing our "self" for us. The same can apply to schoolwork, friendships, conflicts with teachers or whatever they're doing with their hair this week.

Motivation works when it is meaningful to the child, so different kids will respond to different motivators, just

like adults. But some parents resent the need for motivation. "Why should I have to motivate my kid? Why can't
they just do it because they should?" The truth is that
none of us do things because we "should" because behind
every "should" is a need for some payoff. We do what we
do because we get joy from the task; because we're trying
to impress someone; because we want to get paid or recognized; because it's consistent with our value system
and it helps us feel good about ourselves; because we
want to avoid a confrontation or penalty; because we want
the rest of the day free to play; because we want to go to
heaven when we die.

There are no choices without some conscious or uncon-
scious consideration of outcomes. If the task itself isn't
meaningful or rewarding, it will get done only if there is
some other contingency connected to it. At some point,
the motivation may become more intrinsic. One day your
kids may do all the things you'd love them to do because
the chores become a part of who they are. But until then,
your kids may need something else, even something unrelated, to get them going. It takes a while for new behaviors to become intrinsically meaningful and habitual, if
they ever do.

So we can let go of the idea that motivation is bad. It's
true that some *motivators* are bad (like motivating with
abuse), excessive (like buying a kid a car for mowing the
lawn) or simply redundant (like offering additional reward
to a kid who would find the task itself rewarding). And
it's true that we could look at anything outside of pure
intrinsic motivation as bribery, which it is, but certainly
no more so than "bribing" a kid to do what we want with
our love or our fists.

As relationships between parents and kids become increasingly healthy and respectful, the need for you to
motivate your kids will decrease. They are more likely to
see themselves as part of the team and less likely to behave
uncooperatively since their needs are being met in far
more positive ways.

EXERCISE

In what ways did your own parents use negative reactions (e.g., anger, shaming, lectures, violence, disapproval) to motivate you to do what they wanted?

_____

_____

_____

How did you respond to their use of negative reactions?

_____

_____

_____

How have these experiences shaped your behavior as a parent?

_____

_____

_____

In what ways have you used anger and conditional approval to motivate your own children?

_____

_____

_____

What other positive or negative motivators have you used?

_____

_____

Which of these motivators were most effective?

_____

_____

What else motivates your kids? (You might want to ask your children directly for this information.)

_____

_____

_____

Which of these motivators would you be willing to build contingencies upon?

_____

_____

To which tasks would you connect the payoffs to these contingencies?

_____

_____

Nineteen

Negotiate

Motivation and empowerment will eliminate many conflicts from your life. But not all conflicts are issues of motivation and empowerment. Let's say you and your child have been operating under a particular curfew time. It's been working okay, but one day your kid complains that the curfew is too early. What do you do?

Obviously there are a few factors to consider. How long has it been since you agreed to the current curfew? Is his request reasonable? Most important, what's his track record like?

If he hasn't been consistent about coming in on time, refilling the gas tank or fulfilling your initial agreement, he's not ready for additional privileges. You might want to offer him a period of time to prove himself, maybe a month or two at minimum, before you'll be open to discussion. At this point, the agreement is not negotiable.

If he proposes a time that you can live with, say an hour later than what it has been, you might simply agree, particularly if he's been handling the previous agreement responsibly. In that case, there's no real need to negotiate.

But what if he insists that he's older, more responsible and doesn't really need a curfew or wants one that is way beyond anything you could live with? What if it's just for one special occasion? (He might even throw in the old standby about being the only person in his high school who still has a curfew.) You know he's trustworthy, responsible and has never blown it in the past, but there's no way in the world you could agree comfortably.

Maybe it's time to deal.

WATCH YOUR FIRST IMPULSE

Now I know your first impulse might be to scream, "Are you out of your mind? You must think I'm crazy!" However, this response is neither respectful nor particularly effective in resolving conflicts. Your best bet will probably be, first of all, to remain calm, and secondly, to not say much of anything. In fact, if you do say anything, just acknowledge what he's asked you: "Hmm. You want to blow off the curfew this weekend."

You're not agreeing to anything, or making a judgment. This is simply a way of letting him know that you've heard his request. You can even validate this desire: "I understand why you'd like to stay out for such a big event."

Then your boundary: "What you're proposing won't work for me."

And, perhaps, a counteroffer: "I think I could live with a two-hour extension for Friday night."

Listen to his arguments — and there *will* be arguments if your kid is doing his job. If he makes a good case and you can go further: "You know, that sounds pretty reasonable and you've certainly shown that you're responsible. That's still too late for me, but I will agree to (whatever time) as long as the other curfew rules apply. I won't agree to anything later than that." That's your final offer. He may not be particularly happy with it. But having had a chance to present his side, to be heard and taken seriously, and to end up with something closer to what he wanted will make your offer more attractive and easier for him to agree to.

Some kids are born negotiators. One parent said that when her daughter wanted roller blades, she started by asking for a motorcycle and worked her way down to something safer and more affordable. You know your kids. When you ask, "What did you have in mind?" some are going to be straightforward and depend on the reasonableness of their request to gain your consent. Others are going to shoot for the moon.

KNOW YOUR BOUNDARIES

In either case, it's important to know your boundaries. If you're not sure, tell them, "You caught me a little off guard here. I need some time to think about this. Let's talk about it after dinner (in an hour, tomorrow)."

Negotiations can protect the relationship. One single mother negotiated the end of a war over washing the dinner dishes by offering to do all kitchen duty — cooking, setting the table and cleaning up — if her two kids would take over three other chores she normally did. The kids agreed and everyone ended up pitching in, proving they *could* be productive and cooperative as long as dishes were not involved. More important, this win-win solution ended a great deal of stress, conflict and negative interactions in the relationship.

Another mother decided it was time for her 12-year-old son to become involved in the upkeep of the house. She regretted having waited so long and dreaded the confrontation, but she figured it would only get more difficult the longer she put it off. She made a list of 20 things for him to do each week. They were small, manageable and easy-to-do things, nearly all of which involved keeping his own stuff clean and organized. His reaction was predictable: twenty items makes an awfully long list for a kid who has never been responsible for much of anything. The mother compromised: "You know, that *is* quite a lot. Tell you what. Get any 18 done by the end of the week, I'll do the other two and you can have the weekend off." And it worked, if only because the kid got a tremendous amount of power from deciding — and not doing — the two "yuck-iest" jobs on the list.

You can also negotiate commitments from kids who have been having a hard time following through on responsibilities. The parents of a 17-year-old girl were becoming increasingly frustrated by the fact that their daughter consistently neglected to give either parent telephone messages that would come in while she was home. The parents complained and nagged, but nothing changed until they sat down with her and told her that using the telephone is a privilege. They explained, "With that privilege come certain responsibilities, like taking messages for the other people in the household and seeing that we get them. That's not happening now. We need to make different arrangements for sharing the telephone that will work better for all of us. So before you can use the phone again, we need a plan from you in writing. One that tells us how you intend to make sure we get our messages. *All* of our messages. What you will write them down on and where you will keep them until we get home. We don't care how long it takes for you to work this out. You can have your phone privileges back as soon as you have a plan we can all agree on."

Note the tone of this message. There are no judgments, no put-downs and no attempts to disempower. In fact, the only message here is that the current arrangements are not working and that it's the responsibility of the *child* to come up with a better way, one that will accommodate everyone. The payoff for a workable plan was access to the telephone again. By the way, this approach was successful; the parents report that they haven't had problems getting their messages since their daughter made a commitment to writing down every message, or allowing the answering machine to record messages on any calls that weren't for her, until she could afford her own phone line.

Negotiation is terrifically empowering. It's a great tool for building communication and understanding, and for generating commitment. It's a powerful strategy for resolving conflict. And it's a skill your kids will use throughout their lives — to take care of themselves in their personal relationships and in relationship to the rest of the world.

EXERCISE

Describe an area of conflict with your children that might be resolved by negotiating better solutions.

_____

_____

What does your child want in the situation?

_____

_____

What do you want in the situation?

_____

_____

In this conflict, which issues are negotiable for you?

_____

_____

Which issues are not negotiable for you?

_____

_____

What have you tried so far to solve this conflict?

_____

_____

What happened as a result of these efforts to resolve the conflict?

_____

_____

What else might you try to create a win-win solution to this conflict?

_____

_____

Create a statement in the space below that expresses your boundaries without attacking, disempowering or asking your kids to caretake your feelings. What do you need? What are you willing to give in return?

_____

_____

_____

_____

Let Go

Remember that old saying "You can lead a horse to water but you can't make him drink"? This is just a cute way of reminding us that we can do everything "right" and still be disappointed by how things — or people — turn out. As far as kids go, there are many arenas in which our control and influence are limited, and as kids mature, our influence diminishes. This is part of the process by which kids become independent, self-reliant individuals. But when parents begin to experience this phenomenon, certainly by the time the kids hit adolescence, they often respond either by tightening the reins or by giving up completely. Neither of these options provides the support or space kids need to stretch and grow, and both can actually impede the process. The alternative is letting go, which is not at all the same as giving up.

Letting go is about accepting things you can't control, or at least realizing that in any relationship these things do exist. Even if you teach your kids about nutrition, for example, prepare healthy meals and minimize the amount of junk food you bring in to the house, you can still end up with kids who would be quite content to live on Milk Duds, chips and soda. You can demonstrate outstanding organizational skills, provide all kinds of hooks, shelves and containers for their stuff and help them get everything set up, but still find their rooms back in total chaos within 24 hours.

LEARNING VALUES

No matter how thoroughly and effectively you model and teach your values, your kids may not care about certain things that are important to you until later in their lives, if ever. Unfortunately, it's not always possible to get kids to value nutrition, organization, punctuality, cleanliness, learning or whatever. But it is much easier to live with these kids when you can let go. They may miss events because of tardiness, lose things because of disorganization, flunk courses because of poor study habits or not be welcome at the dinner table until they bathe, and they *still* may not seem to care nearly as much as you do. However, letting go enough to allow these consequences to happen can be far more effective in shaping your children's value systems — and subsequent behaviors — than all of your attempts to indoctrinate and control. (Keep in mind that for many kids, indifference is an effective tool for getting attention, hurting back or just staying safe. In many instances, a healthy home environment can eliminate the need for a lot of indifference.)

Letting go helps kids build self-management — a trait we all claim to want kids to have — and it can only happen when we let go and give kids space to manage themselves. Of course they'll make poor choices, especially if we've been controlling and managing their choices for them all along. But in the end, those choices may be the best teachers your kids will ever have.

YOUR NEED TO LOOK GOOD

The obstacle in this process is more likely to be your own need to look good than the persistence of your children's sloppiness, stubbornness or lack of interest. Many parents are reluctant to let go because they are afraid of how their children's choices will reflect their upbringing. Often, we end up enabling our kids — bailing them out and interfering with opportunities for learning — because if we don't pick up their laundry, see that it gets washed and make sure they look clean when they leave the house, we worry about what other people will think of us as parents. Part of letting go is being able to live with the fact that some people may disapprove of our parenting behaviors (although that is certain to happen no matter which parenting behaviors we choose).

Letting go does not mean not caring. It does not mean abandoning kids or throwing them into the deep end so they learn how to swim. Despite letting go, we are still very much present in our relationships with our kids and present in their lives to provide guidance and support. However, we are not in their lives to think for them, to prevent them from making mistakes or to protect them from the results of their choices.

By letting go, you safeguard your boundaries because it allows consequences to happen, and this allows people to learn.

At the risk of beating this example to death, let's go back to the laundry situation. You've set a boundary: you're only washing what's in the hamper and you're only doing it at a specific time each week. You let your family know ahead of time. There is a clear and specific payoff for cooperating. But if your family is used to having you wash the clothes *and* collect them from the floor, the back of the chair and under the bed, it's possible that they may not take you seriously — especially if you've set this boundary before and never bothered to change your behavior. In the past there has never been a reason for them to use the hamper. They might have had to listen to you complain or yell, but up until this point it was simply the small price they had to pay for having their laundry collected and washed for them.

When you can let go enough to maintain your boundaries, the consequences will, no doubt, surprise the people who violate them. But letting go allows *you* to live with the consequences that other people experience. In this case it frees you to stick to your boundaries even if it means that your kids won't have clean clothes (you're probably going to wind up with some very light loads, at least at first).

You no longer need to yell, shame or threaten. If your kids complain, you don't need to say, "I told you so." You simply restate your boundary: "I did what was in the hamper. I'll do the same thing next Saturday at nine."

TRUST THE PROCESS

Letting go means trusting the process enough to know that eventually your kids will need clean clothes badly enough to either start putting them in a place where they will be washed or learn how to run the washer themselves. Maybe both.

Letting go gives you the strength to withhold positive outcomes of agreements with your kids until they complete their part of the bargain. It allows you to let your kids work out their differences with friends, siblings or even their teachers, knowing you're in their corner to support (not rescue) them. It frees you to allow your daughter to miss a movie because her chores weren't done on time, lose a job because she overslept or incur the anger of a relative she forgot to send a thank-you note. It releases you from the inclination to lie or cover for your son when he gets into trouble outside the home. And it will let you hurt inside while all this is going on, without interfering with your children's growth or attacking them for messing up. This gives you space to love, accept and support them so that they'll make more productive choices in the future.

The more attached we are to specific outcomes and expectations for other people, the more difficult it is to let go. In fact, if a child's grades, appearance or the condition of his room is a source of shame for us, it has nothing to do with the child. This is about our need to control, our need to live up to a certain picture of parenthood and our need to get someone else's approval. But it is also an opportunity to explore our own patterns of enmeshment and to separate and disengage where necessary.

Letting go means trusting your child's innate wisdom, despite an apparent lack of evidence of its existence. It means knowing that he will eventually end up where he's supposed to be, even if he takes a rather circuitous route to get there.

EXERCISE

Identify three areas of conflict in your relationship with your child.

1. _____

2. _____

3. _____

For each example of conflict, describe how you would like to see your child behave.

1. _____

2. _____

3. _____

For each example of conflict, tell how this would benefit or pay off for your child.

1. _____

2. _____

3. _____

For each example of conflict, tell how this would benefit or pay off for you. (In other words, what is your attachment to the outcomes you described in the last question?)

1. _____

2. _____

3. _____

Of the outcomes just described, identify the one you would be most willing to let go.

_____

_____

What do you suppose might happen if you simply let go of this outcome?

_____

_____

How can you accomplish this goal of letting go of the outcome? (What actions will you need to take? What kind of support might you need?)

_____

_____

What do you think your child might learn if this happens?

_____

_____

How can you support your child in this conflict without interfering in his learning experience?

_____

_____

Twenty-one

Follow Through

Any boundary worth its salt carries the implication that it is to be taken seriously: You really *will* refuse to make dinner until the countertops are clear; you really *will* withhold telephone privileges until your child has a plan for getting you your messages and you really *will* be available to discuss a problem, but *only* when your child is willing to do so without screaming or name-calling. This is why letting go is such an important part of the process — it's the part that makes following through possible. Unless you are able to let go and let consequences occur, you will inevitably allow your boundaries to be sabotaged by every poor choice your children make.

Following through communicates that you mean what you say. It happens when you do what you say you're going to do or refuse to fulfill your part of the bargain until the other person fulfills hers. Following through helps kids learn to take us seriously. It's the part of the process that demonstrates a boundary is, indeed, a boundary. As a result, following through helps kids experience and recognize the connection between their choices and the results of their choices, which builds responsibility and self-management.

If the child respects your boundary and experiences positive consequences — like being able to borrow your clothes, go out with a friend, have a meal prepared for her, continue a discussion with you that's important to her or use the car again next weekend — she learns how that choice works for her. If the boundary is violated, the positive consequences do not occur. Hopefully your child will think, "Gee, this isn't quite what I wanted. What do I need to do differently next time?" But she will only experience these outcomes — and the learning that goes with them — if you follow through.

A FURTHER CHALLENGE

Although it can take some of us months to realize that we *need* to set a boundary and even more time to gather the courage to express it, that is actually the easy part. Following through can present a much greater challenge, especially for parents who have a history of rescuing or protecting their children from consequences.

One father I worked with complained about constantly having to bail his son out of one financial crisis or another. The boy had bought a car while he was working, but was unable to maintain the job for long. Soon the father was covering the kid's car payments and insurance premiums, as well as the frequent tickets and repair bills. This went on for months, at great financial and emotional expense. The relationship suffered as a result of the father's nagging, criticizing and complaining, but as long as the father kept paying the bills nothing changed.

From the outside, the solution might seem obvious. But every time this father came close to setting a boundary, one that would demand his son to assume some responsibility in the situation, he would immediately begin to worry. "How will he get to school? He hates the bus! What will happen to his grades? He'll drop out and become a bum. I'll have to take care of him for the rest of his life."

Additionally this man loved his son and knew how important the car was to him.

But he was experiencing a nagging suspicion that some of the irresponsible behavior he was seeing — and feeling increasingly angry about — was being encouraged by his own behavior. He was also getting the feeling that his son probably would not change his behavior significantly on his own.

Finally the father changed what he could: his approach to the problem. He calmly told his son that he was no longer willing to pay for his car expenses. "Owning a car is a big responsibility, and I think that all the 'help' I've been giving you has prevented you from assuming this responsibility. Since I've been doing this for a while, I don't think it would be fair to just pull the plug on you. I'll give you another month. That's one more car payment and one more check to the insurance company. Gas, fines, repairs or anything else is up to you from here on out."

Now this kid was no fool. He pulled out every trick that had ever worked for him before. But his father stood firm. "One more month."

"But what if I can't get a job? I might lose the car."

"Yes, you might."

"Then how do you expect me to get a job or get to school?"

"I don't know. But I believe you'll work something out."

As wrenching as this all was for the father, getting to this point and actually communicating the boundary was, indeed, the easy part. The hard part was living within the boundary he had set, being willing to allow his child to create his own solution to the problem, even if it meant losing the car in the process.

BE CONSISTENT

Hopefully, the consequences of the boundaries you set will be far less dramatic than the previous example. It's always easier to prevent a problem than it is to back out of one you've been contributing to. But either way, you will be tested. Count on it. In fact, hope for it. It will be a great chance for you to practice behaviors that are consistent with the boundaries you set. And it will be a great learning experience for your kids.

For example, you can operate successfully for months on the contingency that the car is only available next weekend if your daughter brings it in on time this weekend. The one time your kid comes in late will be the week before the big game or the prom. Will you have the courage and commitment to follow through? Because as soon as you start making excuses for your kids or encouraging them to give you excuses (in the hope that if they're creative or pathetic enough, you can relax the boundaries "just this once"), you'll be reinforcing the idea that you don't deserve to be taken seriously. Respecting your own boundaries is a prerequisite to generating respect from others.

So be careful that you don't set boundaries you're not prepared to follow through on. Make sure that your children know exactly how firm your boundaries are. One parent negotiated an 11 o'clock curfew with her son. She clarified that this meant 11 o'clock by her watch and that 11:01 was past curfew.

"What if I get a flat?" he asked.

"I hope you can get it fixed in time to be home by eleven," the mother answered.

Think your boundaries through. If you allow your kids to borrow your clothes, what responsibilities go along with that privilege? Do they have to ask you first? How soon do they have to return what they borrow? Are they responsible for laundering or for paying the dry cleaning bills? Which items are okay to borrow and which are off limits? What are their financial responsibilities if an item is damaged? Have they agreed to all of these conditions beforehand?

VIOLATIONS ARE OPPORTUNITIES

Boundary violations present opportunities to build the relationship, although it may not seem obvious at the time. Following through allows you to depersonalize consequences when a boundary has been breached. You don't need to get aggravated and you don't need to attack, punish or take revenge. You simply need to follow through, leaving the door open for your child to get it right next time. Instead of handling a broken agreement with, "Well, you really blew it big time, Bucko. Let's see how soon you get to use the car again," try something like, "I see our curfew agreement didn't work out this weekend. Let's try again in two weeks (or whatever time frame you've previously agreed to)." An approach that states, "This isn't working," suggests that there is a flaw in the choices or commitment, rather than a flaw in the child (which, incidentally, is far more difficult to "fix.")

Does this mean you won't encounter conflict? Of course not, although the more consistently you hold to your boundaries, the more unnecessary conflict becomes. If your kids are used to getting their way with whining, arguing, begging or making excuses, they've learned that you've got some pretty "mushy" boundaries. This is what has worked for them in the past. Why would they stop now? You may even have to explain, as one parent did, "I understand why you're so upset. I haven't been very consistent with my limits in the past. It's probably confusing that I'm holding us both to our agreement now. It's even a little unsettling for me. But I believe we'll both get better at this."

It *does* get better, eventually. There's something strangely reassuring about hearing, "Dinner is whatever you fix for yourself tonight. I'll cook tomorrow if the counters are clean by five." There's a certain predictability about this one piece of their lives: they *do* have to do their part if they want to have their meals prepared for them, and they *will* have meals prepared when they do their part.

COMMIT TO WINNING

In the meantime, you might have to live with their reaction, but the less afraid you become of their anger or criticism, the faster they'll realize how pointless their reactivity is. When you show a commitment to having everyone "win," there is a greater payoff for cooperation than for trying to make you lose.

There are other outcomes you might have to live with. These range from the possibility that they might eat something less nutritional than you'd like to the possibility that they might create even more of a mess than you started with. In the latter case, you will need some new boundaries about which foods, utensils or appliances are available when they have to fix meals on their own.

Causing Problems For Others

There is also the possibility that one person's sloppiness or lack of cooperation will create problems — in this case, no dinner being prepared — for people who did not contribute to the mess. One parent found peer pressure and teamwork to be incredibly effective when she stuck to her boundary and left the rest of the family to work out a solution among themselves. (Think of this in terms of another example: If one person delays a group of people and, as a result, the entire group gets to the store late, does the store open up for the people who would have been on time otherwise? Of course not. It becomes necessary for the group to solve that problem. It has nothing to do with the store.)

If the behavior doesn't improve or if the pattern is one of agreements continually being broken, you may need to renegotiate a commitment and change the outcomes. It will give your kids more of a stake in cooperating if you ask for some evidence that they understand what the agreement calls for. You'll run into problems if the boundary is unclear, unrealistic or extremely unreasonable, or if the boundary was "called" in a moment of anger, intended more as a punishment or source of revenge than as an actual boundary. Remember, boundaries consider everyone's needs. If you've set something up that was intended to hurt or disempower, back up and start again. But be prepared to follow through.

Sometimes kids blow it because they haven't learned any better, and sometimes just to see if you really mean it. Either way, their experiences are capable of teaching them to make more cooperative choices. This occurs only when you take yourself seriously enough to respect your own boundaries. And that means following through.

EXERCISE

In what instances have you been successful in allowing your children to experience positive consequences for respecting a boundary?

_____

_____

What was the outcome of allowing your children to experience positive consequences for respecting a boundary?

_____

_____

In what instances have you been successful in restricting positive consequences when a boundary was violated?

_____

_____

What was the outcome of restricting positive consequences when a boundary was violated?

_____

_____

In what instances have you relaxed or rescinded a boundary that your child violated? (In other words, in what instances have you allowed positive consequences to occur, even though your child did not hold up his or her end of the bargain?)

_____

_____

What prompted you to invalidate your own boundary?

_____

_____

What was the outcome of relaxing this boundary?

_____

_____

Which of your boundaries do your children respect the most?

_____

_____

Why do you suppose they respect these boundaries more than others?

_____

_____

Which of your boundaries do your children violate or disregard the most?

_____

_____

Why do you suppose they violate or disregard these boundaries more than others?

_____

_____

What might you do differently to ensure that your children will respect these boundaries in the future?

_____

_____

_____

Twenty-two

Reorient

Some people never seem to have anything positive to say. Whether they're talking about the weather, their health, other people or life in general, their conversation always emphasizes the negative. That kind of behavior reflects that person's orientation to life: how that person regards the state of the world and on what that person tends to focus.

The same can be said of families. The ability to orient one's thinking in positive directions is a critical ingredient of boundary-setting. Positivity plays a large part in the dynamics of healthy families. If the adults who were present in your life as a child were basically positive people, you have an idea of how this works. But without the role models that a healthy family can provide, a positive orientation to life can be hard to come by.

KEEP A POSITIVE FOCUS

Nonetheless, even with great role models a positive focus is often an early casualty of the demands of day-to-day living and this affects the quality of our relationships.

119

Did you ever wonder, at the end of a particularly exasperating day, if you managed to say one nice thing to your kids? Do you often go to bed feeling as if all you did all day was yell, criticize and complain? Do you tend to notice what's wrong with something before you notice what's right? When you set boundaries, do you stress the negative consequences the kids will face if they mess up, or do you focus on the positive outcomes for cooperation? Have you ever made a sincere commitment to be more positive in your interactions with your son, only to have your best intentions dissolve the moment you trip over the soccer gear he left in the hall?

We come by this orientation honestly. To a great extent, orientation was learned from the adults in our lives when we were growing up, from the feedback we got on our papers in school, from other people we saw around us and even from the news on TV. But orientation is not a function of external forces. Instead, it is a personal choice and commitment we make internally, external influences notwithstanding. Even though negativity can be hard to avoid, the orientation and the habits it inspires can be avoided, even unlearned. In fact, reorienting to the positive may be one of the simplest and most concrete changes you can make in your relationships with your kids. And it doesn't even matter how they look, talk or act.

THE NEGATIVE ATTITUDE

When your orientation is negative, most of what you see when you look at your children — their rooms, their clothing, their homework or their friends, for example — will be negative. You will notice the one thing they forgot to put away when they cleaned their rooms. You will see the hairstyle you hate, the spot on the shirt or the holes in the jeans. When you read the letters or stories they write, you will see mistakes and misspellings before you notice content or creativity. You may, in the heat of battle, lose all sight of anything good about your children as they suddenly become "people who never write thank-you notes." And you will probably see this as perfectly normal. In fact, you may even see this as your job.

Parents sometimes worry that their kids won't mature without criticism, without someone to point out mistakes in their judgment or logic, or without someone to let them know when they are wrong. It seems as if focusing on the positive means accepting, even condoning, the negative. This is more all-or-nothing thinking at work. A positive focus does not interfere with your ability to demonstrate alternatives, offer suggestions, lend a hand, correct misinformation and intervene in potentially dangerous or destructive situations. A positive focus allows you to do these things without shaming or attacking your children, without making them wrong or without violating their sense of worth.

In fact, the kind of "growth" that comes from shame, guilt, fear or self-hatred is hardly what most of us want for our kids. The result of consistent criticism and negative feedback tends to be a shallow, impermanent form of self-protection with by-products such as perfectionism, low self-esteem and a sense of inadequacy. Yet there is a tendency in some families for parents to rationalize hurtful behavior as a legitimate attempt to "toughen up" their kids to prepare them for life.

It's true many people appear successful even though they grew up in unspeakably negative environments. But what did it cost them? Constructive change and development happen in an atmosphere of healthy, loving relationships. Part of this atmosphere is an orientation to positivity and success — what your children need *now* to develop the confidence, flexibility and resilience they'll need down the road. Repeatedly knocking them down isn't the answer (because after a while, even healthy kids stop bothering to get up). A far less destructive way to achieve the same goal is to create a positive environment in which the consequences of taking risks and making bad choices don't threaten your children's safety or worth.

As you incorporate more and more healthy behaviors into your relationships with your children, you reduce the need for criticism and negative feedback. After a while, your unconditional acceptance and respect, coupled with your ability to separate and let go, will get you past your children's hair or clothes, if you even notice them at all anymore. Since behaviors like anticipation, cooperation, negotiation and follow-through will lead to boundaries that only allow privileges under certain conditions, you don't need to nag or threaten until those conditions are met.

Positivity represents far more than the reduction of stress, conflict and negativity in relationships. It's also a conscious and deliberate part of the relationship-building process that can inspire other positive outcomes. For example, let's look at contingencies and the way we express them.

On one hand, we can connect what we want with what the kid wants by a threat: "You are not going away next weekend unless your chores are done." On the other hand, we can communicate the same connection with a promise: "Next weekend sounds like fun. As long as your chores are done, you can go." The connection between the chores and the privilege of going away is the same, but there is a big difference both in the way these two statements operate and in the emotional climate they create.

PROMISES

Promises reflect a simple, but profound, shift in the dynamics of a relationship. While threats focus on negative consequences, stating contingencies in terms of the parent's power ("Do it or else"), promises offer the child power by focusing on the positive outcomes of cooperative choices, *their* choices. Promises are therefore less likely to evoke rebelliousness and resistance. While the implication of a negative consequence still exists, there is no disempowerment or violation of the child. Sure, it's subtle. But it works, if for no other reason than promises are just more pleasant to hear.

Promises also take the responsibility off the parents' shoulders and places it back with the child. One couple changed their contingency from "If your homework isn't done by 8:00, you can't use the phone" to "sure you can use the phone from 8:00 to 9:00 as long as your homework is done beforehand." Their daughter became upset instantly, saying, "That isn't fair! Now I won't be able to blame you anymore!"

Promises reflect a pro-active reward orientation, emphasizing the payoff for cooperation (rather than punishment for noncompliance). This represents a major departure from the way most families operate. In fact, in my work with parents, the questions I hear most often begin with "What do I do when . . ." followed by some misbehavior perpetrated by the child. Actually no one has ever asked, "How do I take revenge on the little jerk when he gets detention six nights in a row?" But the concerns most frequently expressed in these families reflect an environment of reactivity and an orientation to punishment for misdeeds. This is, after all, a model that is so familiar and pervasive that it seems to exclude any alternative: The kid messes up, the parents enforce a penalty.

But there is an alternative: an environment of prevention and reward orientation in which your home becomes a place where "good things happen when . . ." instead of a place where negative consequences are stressed. Even though your kids may not always have access to these rewards or positive results, it's only because they haven't come through on their end. The rewards, whether clean laundry, cooked meals, a ride to the mall, one's allowance, TV privileges, use of the car or even the ability to continue to live in the house, still exist. They just require a different set of behaviors on the part of the child. And in a positively-oriented home, kids have a lot of space to explore different behaviors until they get it right.

Yet despite all this, there will be days when the world feels like a very negative place. As we bog down in the drama of daily living, a positive focus on the world can be hard to hold onto. But making a deliberate effort to focus on the positive has implications for our mental health, our physical well-being and the quality of our relationships. And that can make the challenges of dealing with our lives — and the people in them — a lot easier to face.

EXERCISE

When you were growing up, was the bulk of the feedback you got from your parents positive or negative?

Even if the feedback was predominantly positive, what types of negative messages did you receive?

What effect did these negative messages have on you?

How do you think negative messages have affected your parenting?

Keep track of the critical or negative comments you make for the next day or two. In what ways were you critical of your children (their attitudes, their rooms or possessions, their personalities, their behavior, their grades, their language, their appearance or the things they like)?

In what ways were you critical or negative about people your children know?

_____

_____

In what ways were you critical or negative about people or the world in general?

_____

_____

What was your intention in providing this negative feedback?

_____

_____

How did these interactions affect the quality of the relationship?

_____

_____

What might you do differently next time?

_____

_____

In what ways is your home punishment-oriented?

_____

_____

In what ways is your home reward-oriented?

_____

_____

Write out three threats you have made to your children. (These are negatively stated contingencies that may start out "If you don't . . ."; "If I catch you . . ." or "If you're not . . ." for example.)

1. _____

2. _____

3. _____

Rewrite each of the previously stated threats as a promise. (These are positively stated contingencies that may start out "As soon as . . ."; "When you finish . . ." or "You can . . ." for example.)

1. _____

2. _____

3. _____

Identify two things you plan to do in the next 24 hours to demonstrate positivity in your relationship with your children, no matter what else happens.

1. _____

2. _____

Twenty-three

Acknowledge

A funny thing happens when we make a conscious decision to look for the positive in the people and things around us. We actually start noticing the good, sometimes even to the exclusion of flaws and imperfections. This orientation creates opportunities for us to practice yet another healthy behavior in our dealings with kids: acknowledgment.

Acknowledgment means letting people know we value and appreciate them, that we recognize their efforts and achievements and that we see the good in who they are. This ingredient is widely recommended as a means of encouragement, recognition and building self-esteem. But like anything else in adult-child relationships, there are things to watch out for.

NOT CHANGING OR CONTROLLING

Perhaps the most important aspect of an honest acknowledgment is that it is not intended to change or control the other person. It is simply meant to recognize. Unfortunately, a lot of manipulative interactions masquerade as honest acknowledgments.

Take praise, for instance. Praise is indeed a way of acknowledging someone. The problem with praise is that it invariably contains an element of approval or judgment that ties worth to behavior: "You're so good for cleaning your room"; "I'm so proud of you for making the team" or "I love you when you get good grades!"

Now these sentences may sound harmless or even extremely positive. Most of us make approval-type statements in complete innocence and sincerity. They'll certainly get my vote over criticism, shaming, put-downs or name-calling. But there is still a shadow of criticism that implies that the child's value depends on his behavior: "You're *not* good when your room is a mess"; "I *wouldn't* be proud of you if you hadn't made the team" and "I *don't* love you when your grades aren't good." Since it's doubtful that you really feel this way, why take the chance of communicating something you really don't mean? There are better ways.

If you've been working on establishing an environment of unconditional love and acceptance, your kids are probably less vulnerable to the occasional approval statement because they are learning that they are valued no matter what. But even verbal expressions of these positive feelings can be miscommunicated.

For example, the words "I love you" convey unconditional love, but only when we don't attach them to something that is conditional, like the child's behavior, appearance or performance. "I love you" is a complete sentence that can be stated unconditionally, out of the blue and unconnected to anything the other person has said or done. If you're not used to saying it, write it in a note. If your kids aren't used to hearing it, tell them again. And again. Make it a fact of your relationship, regardless of anything else that is happening. If you hear yourself attaching words like "when" or "because," you are probably setting up a statement of conditional love.

ELIMINATE "BUT"

It's the people-pleasing part of us that says things like "I love you, but . . .," the part that is afraid to set a boundary or confront directly whatever comes after "but." Rarely will your love have anything to do with the problem, or even the solution, so don't burden the process. Deal with the issue directly: "I'm not comfortable with that expression. Please don't use it around me anymore." Leading in with, "I love you, but . . ." is an attempt to soften the conflict and make yourself less vulnerable to any repercussions you fear for standing up for yourself. Even if your children accuse you of not loving them because you aren't willing to do something and you feel compelled to clarify, try dropping the word "but." For example, "Of course I love you. In fact that's part of the reason I refuse to write a note to get you out of that test."

It's probably a good idea to keep the word "but" out of all of your acknowledgments. When our brains hear the word "but," they automatically cancel anything that was said up to that point. So when you make a statement like, "You're hair looks great but those pants are horrible," chances are the only thing your kid hears is the part about the pants. Actually, you don't even need to mention the pants. If your child asks for your opinion and you really don't like the pants, you can certainly respond, but be careful not to attack your kid. ("I like the black ones better" is easier to take than "What were you on when you got dressed?" By the way, if you immediately started thinking, "But I couldn't let him go out in those pants!" you might want to back up a few chapters and reread the section on letting go.)

WATCH MANIPULATIVE COMPLIMENTS

Watch, too, for a tendency to compliment another person in an attempt to get someone to change: "Joshua is such a nice boy. I understand he visits his grandfather every Sunday," or, "But your sister is so good in science." Also beware of using a compliment as an opportunity to criticize something else: "You're doing so well in math. Why can't you keep up in music?" Or my personal favorite, "You have such a pretty face. If you only lost a few pounds you'd look great." Attempts to flatter someone into doing something we want ultimately will be ineffective and transparent to all except those most desperate for our approval.

Acknowledgment is a means of expressing a positive focus. It relies neither on completion nor perfection. Even if your child has done only two of three chores, you can recognize progress with something like, "Hey, great start!" or "You're almost done." Don't forget, if a reward or privilege is contingent on completing all three chores, you don't need to comment on the chore that's not finished. The absence of the reward will be comment enough and, in the meantime, your acknowledgment can be very encouraging.

RECOGNITION STATEMENTS

Although actually experiencing positive outcomes is most effective strengthing and reinforcing positive behavior, verbal recognition can help. Recognition statements, which focus on the child's behavior as opposed to his worth as a human being, are excellent alternatives to praise or approval statements. In addition, they verbally connect his choices to the positive outcomes, reinforcing the power he has to impact his life in positive ways.

Recognition statements happen after a boundary has been established and the child has completed her part of the agreement. These statements contain two parts. The first part describes the behavior: "Hey, I see you washed and ironed that blouse you borrowed." See how this differs from praise, which emphasizes the child's worth with a statement like, "You are so wonderful!" (Isn't your child wonderful and worthwhile whether or not you ever get your blouse back?)

The second part tells the child how her behavior will pay off for her. If you have set up a boundary ahead of time that makes laundering and returning borrowed clothes a contingency for future clothes-borrowing privileges, then this part will be easy: "You can borrow it again any time, so long as you ask first." (Notice that the payoff does not attempt to project emotional payoffs onto the child. It's presumptuous to acknowledge this with a statement like, "You must feel proud of yourself," or "You should be happy you were so responsible." Focus on the actual outcome.)

While there is obviously a note of appreciation here, a recognition statement focuses *away* from your reaction. This is about your child's actions and the way her choices worked for her. Do you want her to be tied to your pleasure and approval or to be motivated by the chance to borrow your clothes again as a result of her responsible behavior?

There are other healthy and honest ways to acknowledge a child. We can use statements that express appreciation: "You're really neat"; "I really enjoy your sense of humor" or "Thanks for your help. This would have been much more difficult to do without you."

We can recognize achievement or effort: "You did a fine job on that project"; "You handled that very responsibly"; "You've really been working hard this week" or "You may not notice it, but I've seen a real improvement in your writing."

We can acknowledge with genuine admiration: "That color is great on you"; "I like your hair like that" or "You are really quite talented."

And we can acknowledge with actions: a hug, a touch, a smile, a wink, a love note or a special favor.

One last caution: Beware, once again, of all-or-nothing thinking! A mother once called me after a workshop on this topic. She was concerned, she said, because she "almost slipped and gave someone a compliment." Acknowledgments can indeed be complimentary and they can certainly reflect your enthusiasm and appreciation. The acid test is whether or not your comments are intended to change something in the other person's behavior or value system.

Check your intentions with questions like these: Am I saying this to get him to act, look or feel differently? Am I trying to get something from this child? Does it matter how he responds? Do I really mean what I'm saying? If your acknowledgments are genuine and you have no investment in particular outcomes, these statements can contribute a great deal to your relationship, as well as to your image of yourself as a loving parent. So even though these comments might indeed strengthen your child's positive behaviors or self-perception, the person you really say them for is you.

EXERCISE

Identify five things you really appreciate about each of your children. Focus on who they are rather than on the specific things they've done.

Child _____   Child _____

1. _____   1. _____

2. _____   2. _____

3. _____   3. _____

4. _____   4. _____

5. _____   5. _____

Child _____   Child _____

1. _____   1. _____

2. _____   2. _____

3. _____   3. _____

4. _____   4. _____

5. _____   5. _____

How have you expressed your appreciation and love for them within the past week?

_____

_____

_____

What else might you do or say to let them know you appreciate and value them?

_____

_____

_____

Think of three of the contingencies you have set up recently. For each, tell what you want the child to do.

1. _____

2. _____

3. _____

What is the positive outcome the child will experience upon completion of these tasks?

1. _____

2. _____

3. _____

Imagine that your child has just completed the behavior called for in the contingency. Construct a recognition statement you can use that will connect his cooperation to the payoff now available. For each statement, describe what the child has just done ("I see you brought the car back on time") and connect it to the positive outcome ("Now you can have it again next Friday").

1. _____

_____

2. _____

_____

3. _____

_____

Identify two things you plan to do in the next 24 hours to acknowledge your children, no matter what else happens.

1. _____

_____

2. _____

_____

Twenty-Four

Model

Like it or not, you are one of the most influential teachers your children have had. They've seen how you act under pressure and how you behave around different people. They've witnessed your expressions of language, power and feelings. They've observed your value system in your actions. And even if they've fought you every inch of the way, they've learned from all of this.

While they may reject a lot of what they've seen, many of the unchallenged behaviors and belief systems — the things that come most automatically to them — have come from you. This is true even when they deliberately attempt to model people *other* than you. (Think of the times you've heard your own parent's voice come out of your mouth.)

Of course you're not the only person your children learn from. Every year the world seems to get bigger, offering all of us access to more models, influences and information than ever before. Short of locking your kid in a closet, you have limited control over what your children experience outside of their interactions with you. Fortunately, kids pick up some good stuff from parents as

well as a few behaviors you'd prefer never to see, and
your positive influences are among the tools they'll use to
sort through what they see around them.

Let's look at what your children do learn from you. Your
role as parent is your only hope of insuring that at least
one of the models in your children's lives is providing the
kind of information you want them to have, regardless of
what they do with it. But without a little attention, your
modeling can be a source of confusion, mixed messages,
and double standards.

WALK THE TALK

The rule of effective modeling is simple: Walk the talk.
In other words, to the best of your ability, act as you
would have them act. When your children hear you say
one thing and see you do another, they are far more likely
to believe — and learn from — what they see.

Watch the tendency to dismiss certain discrepancies as
simply a function of age differences. Saying that certain
things are okay "when you get to be an adult" can make
those things rather enticing to your kids who have an
investment in proving that they are no longer children.
But the fact is, adults are entitled to — or can sometimes
get away with — certain activities that really are inappropriate, illegal, dangerous or just plain dumb for kids. So
draw your lines carefully. There are no easy answers here,
especially since your behavior legitimizes many of the
choices you'd rather your kids not make.

Are you, for example, as clean and sober as you want
your children to be? With certain substances, such as
tobacco and alcohol, you have the law on your side. But
you also have a greater risk of your kids using those
substances if you do. After a while, it won't make much
sense to your kids that it's not okay for them to do things
that you obviously enjoy. And what kind of messages are
we sending when we use other substances that are no
more legal for us than they are for them?

What about other forms of role modeling? You probably have dozens of opportunities every day to affect your children's learning with the behaviors, language patterns and attitudes you model. For example, what kind of example do you set for character traits such as reliability, punctuality, neatness, honesty, persistence, considerateness or even personal hygiene?

What about your language? Are your kids allowed to use the same words and expressions you do? Can they talk to you in the same tone of voice you use when you speak to them? You'll probably find it difficult to establish a safe, win-win home environment when your behavior is inconsistent with your demands and expectations.

If people call when you don't want to come to the phone, do you tell them that now is not a good time and make arrangements to call them back, or do you pretend you're not home and ask someone in the family to lie for you? Do you misrepresent facts, events or yourself to avoid conflict or make yourself look good? Do you lie for your kids to keep them out of trouble?

What about your sense of responsibility? Do you fulfill promises and obligations reliably? Do you return things you borrow in good condition and on time? Do you repair or replace things you damage? Do you admit to your mistakes, or do you make excuses or blame someone or something else? Do you confront your problems directly or are you prone to triangulation, manipulation or passive-aggressive behavior?

Do you stick up for yourself without hurting others or do you allow people in your life to abuse you, either physically, emotionally or verbally? Do you make excuses for someone else's words or actions?

Are you responsible for your feelings, or do you tell others that they *make* you feel a certain way? Do you hold your kids, your spouse, your parents or your boss accountable for your peace of mind — or the lack thereof?

How do you show concern for the environment? How do you treat animals? What about other people? Are you tolerant and accepting of people who are different from you? How well do you listen? Are you supportive and understanding when others hurt or have problems? Do you gossip? Can you keep a secret?

How important is it for you to be right? Have your relationships suffered because of your need to "win"?

Do you treat your children with the same courtesy and respect you demonstrate to your friends and other adults? Do you react to things your children do that you would probably not even notice if someone else did the same thing? Do you expect a payoff for the things you do — perhaps in the form of recognition, appreciation, reciprocity or maybe a paycheck, promotion or raise — but resent the fact that your children need motivation for the things you want them to do? Any time you operate with a double standard, you're bound to create obstacles in your relationship.

How do you act when you're angry? Do you use your anger to rationalize hurtful behaviors, such as shaming, insulting, blaming or hitting? Or do you use your anger to identify new behaviors for yourself, different ways to approach a problem or places where you need to communicate a boundary that you may have overlooked?

Whatever your answer to any of these questions, your behavior provides a model of ways your children can respond when faced with similar challenges. Are you giving them the messages you want them to hear?

Watch your actions, your language and your attitudes over the next few days. Look for inconsistencies, places where you might be able to bring your behaviors more in line with your expectations for your kids, if for no other reason than to justify wanting the same in return.

For example, perhaps you are one of those parents who quit swearing — at least in your children's presence — from the day they entered your life. However, if your children have spent more than eight seconds outside your home (or in some instances, watching TV), they have been exposed to all kinds of language. Given the influence of peers or TV idols, your children may have started using some of those words and expressions themselves. While you don't have much control over how they talk, your modeling entitles you to ask that they at least refrain from swearing in your presence: "Wait a minute. I don't use that kind of language around you and I'm uncomfortable hearing you use it. Please don't say that word around me anymore." This boundary reflects the value system you have demonstrated through your actions, not your admonitions. In fact, any boundary rooted in the integrity of your own behaviors and belief systems carries a power that simple rules or demands will never have.

So listen for the times you tell your children, "Do as I say, not as I do." No matter *what* you say, the real message they hear is conveyed by your actions.

EXERCISE

Identify five things you do that model behaviors, language patterns or belief systems that you want your children to emulate.

1. _____

2. _____

3. _____

4. _____

5. _____

Which of these behaviors have you seen your children demonstrate?

_____

_____

Identify five things you do that model behaviors, language patterns or belief systems that are inconsistent with those you want your children to emulate.

1. _____

2. _____

3. _____

4. _____

5. _____

Which of these behaviors have you seen your children demonstrate?

_____

_____

Which of these behaviors are you the most willing to notice and change?

_____

_____

What will you do differently?

_____

_____

Twenty-Five

Support

Uh-oh. Your child is having a feeling. Perhaps he's sad, angry or worried. Normal feelings, right? Everyone has them. (Okay, so maybe they're a little more frequent and extreme during adolescence.) There's no question that feelings are a normal part of life. The question is — and this is a challenge for anyone in any relationship — how to best support someone who seems to be going through "something"?

Unless you grew up in a very unusual situation, you probably didn't have many models for dealing with other people's feelings in healthy, supportive ways. In fact, many of us grew up with adults in our lives who were, to some degree, rather uncomfortable with our feelings, if not downright frightened by them. For many of us, the expression of feelings evoked negative, nonsupportive responses that could even be more disconcerting than the feelings themselves. In order to protect ourselves, we may have learned to disconnect from our feelings, hide them or pretend they didn't exist.

To compound this dilemma, the adults in our lives may have used their own feelings to change or control our behavior: "You make me mad!"; "I'm so happy when you do well in school" or "Quiet down or you'll upset your mother."

So in many families, feelings become liabilities for kids and weapons for adults. Either way, the message is clear: Feelings are bad — things that cause problems, things to be protected from. It's no wonder so many of us are uncomfortable with feelings. It is this discomfort that interferes with our ability to provide support, especially to our kids, when they are having feelings.

A SAFE ENVIRONMENT

The ultimate goal of supportiveness is to provide an emotional environment in which it is safe to have feelings. It's not about protecting kids from their feelings or cheering them up when they're unhappy. It's not about fixing whatever is causing their problems. And it's not about using their feelings to teach them a lesson. It's just about letting feelings happen.

Supportiveness allows feelings to be expressed directly ("I'm sad today."), as preferences, desires, opinions ("I hate lima beans!" or "I wish I could have a new car!"), resentments ("How come she gets all the breaks?") or as personal realities ("I'm so bored!" or "I'm scared of thunder."). Often a response isn't even required. Just knowing it's okay to have the feeling may be enough. But how many of us can just hear statements like these without feeling the need to take them personally, get defensive or try to change the person's mind?

At first glance, the patterns we've learned may seem innocent enough. However, many of the responses that *seem* to be supportive actually may compound a child's problems. Certainly the more afraid we are of feelings, the more inadequate we feel when our kids are upset. Or the more we see our role as one of keeping everyone happy, the more difficult it is to respond in a genuinely supportive manner.

Any response that interferes with children's ability to own, experience or process their feelings is not supportive. Nonsupportive responses teach children to mistrust their feelings and perceptions. They interfere with the development of their problem-solving capabilities. And, as if that weren't enough, nonsupportive responses tend to block communications and erode trust in relationships. When your kids do need support and encouragement, don't you want to be the one they feel they can turn to?

MAKING FEELINGS GO AWAY

Nonsupportive responses are boundary violations in which ownership of the feelings, and the responsibility for dealing with the issues surrounding the feelings, can get hopelessly confused. Unfortunately, nonsupportive responses are what we know best, the ones that come almost automatically. Let's look at these responses and see how they can end up working against us, our kids and the relationships we're trying to build.

First of all, there are the kinds of responses that try to get children out of their feelings or make the feelings go away. These responses may be very familiar to adults who try to protect their children from their feelings, or to adults who are especially uncomfortable with their children's feelings. The problem with these responses is that they communicate a lack of respect for what the children are experiencing and put children in the position of having to defend their feelings. These responses reinforce self-doubt and a sense of "wrongness" about having the feelings, compounding the initial problem that is never gets dealt with when we try to make the feelings go away.

Dismissing

We might attempt to make the child's feelings go away by dismissing them. This type of response might sound like "That's nothing to be upset over"; "That doesn't mean anything" or "So she said you were ugly. Big deal!" Certainly some of our kids' traumas may seem pretty frivolous at times, especially if we're having a tough day or we're in the middle of a trauma of our own. Adolescents and teens can be rather dramatic about their problems. They lack the perspective that allows us to see how silly this will all seem a year from now. But to them, whatever they're feeling is very immediate and very real.

Excusing

We may also dismiss a child's feelings by making excuses for the other person's behavior: "He didn't know what he was saying"; "She must be having a bad day" or "Well, her parents are going through a divorce." This may sound reassuring, but when the child has been hurt or abused, making excuses for the people who hurt him conveys a dangerous message that it's okay for the child to be violated.

Denying

Another strategy is to deny the feelings. I've asked dozens of groups of adults what the typical response might be to a child who says, "I hate my sister." Without exception and in unison they reply, "No you don't." These same people may also have said things such as "That's ridiculous. Teachers don't hate their students" or "But he's such a nice man. You don't really feel that way."

We deny children's feelings when we are afraid of the feelings or when the feelings challenge our reality or value system. But responses that deny the validity or reality of a child's feelings, for whatever reasons, can create self-doubt and teach children to mistrust their perceptions.

Distracting

We might also distract children from their feelings, often by focusing on something else: "But you're so good in your other subjects"; "Things could be worse"; "You're lucky you *have* a brother" or "You think *you've* got problems?"

This is the technique we rely on when we're too impatient with — or surprised by — children's feelings; when we can't relate to what they're feeling and experiencing or when we're too wrapped up in our own issues and feelings to be supportive. Distracting distorts the child's reality and can be extremely confusing, even to a fairly sophisticated kid.

Medicating

One of the more dangerous responses when attempting to get the child out of his feelings takes the form of "medicating." Adults who would never think of pouring their kids a shot of whiskey to help ease the pain of not having a date for the prom often think nothing of going out for ice cream to accomplish the same thing. Medicating responses use some type of substance (usually food) or activity (e.g., schoolwork, TV, chores, shopping) to distract children from their feelings.

When we attempt to "medicate" kids, we communicate that it's not only bad to have the feelings, but also that when feelings come up, the natural and correct response is to take something or do something to make the feelings go away. No one would deliberately create this set-up for addiction or compulsive behavior. Yet this response may be automatic, particularly for those of us who have a history of deliberately responding to our own feelings in this way.

Making The Child Wrong

There are other ways to respond nonsupportively. Sometimes we attempt to make the child wrong for having the feelings in the first place. These responses are often expressed in anger, impatience or frustration. They often occur when a child expresses feelings that somehow trigger in us a sense of shame, anger, inadequacy or frustration: "If I were doing a better job as a parent, my kid wouldn't feel this way."

Blaming

Does it make you crazy when kids experience certain feelings that could have been prevented if only they'd listened? Have you ever been tempted to respond with something like, "I told you this would happen!" or "Well, what did you expect?" This nonsupportive strategy is called blaming. Blaming suggests that the child deserves the discomfort he's feeling. This response might sound like: "What did you do to her?"; "Well, if you had just studied!"; "That's what happens when you overeat." or "You never listen." It's very likely that your kid has already figured this out, but even if he hasn't made that connection, right now he needs an "ear", not a cause-and-effect lecture.

These hurtful kinds of responses can just slip out of our mouths when we see a child in pain that probably could have been avoided. Yet blaming, like so many other nonsupportive responses, simply compounds the problem and hurts the relationship. (How likely is it that your child will see you as a safe person to turn to the next time he's upset about something?)

Attacking

Similar to blaming is attacking, which may be expressed as criticism, shaming or judgments: "Don't be a sissy!"; "You're so ungrateful!"; "Nice boys don't hate their sisters!" or "You're just too sensitive!" Even nonverbal impatience, frustration, disappointment or anger are shaming. These responses make a child wrong for having the feelings. They reinforce inadequacy, can provoke defensiveness, demolish self-esteem and are a sure fire way to shut down communications.

Shaming or attacking responses often occur when a child has expressed feelings such as fear, anger, sadness or neediness; but may also occur when a child is feeling joyful, smug or confident: "You think you know everything?" or "Wipe that smile off your face!"

Challenging

Another nonsupportive strategy involves challenging the feelings. "Why does that bother you?" may sound like a supportive response, if only because it seems to demonstrate our interest and intent to listen. But asking children why they're feeling a certain way is also asking them to defend their feelings and their rights to have their feelings. Challenging children communicates that it's only okay to have the feelings as long as the problem is big enough or bad enough. It also communicates that your acceptance of them — and their feelings — is conditional, based on their ability to convince you in some way that their feelings are, indeed, justifiable.

Enmeshing

Then there's a strange type of attacking response called enmeshing that somehow focuses the feelings or the problem back on to the adult's experience. This may sound like, "Well, I never had a problem with math," which has nothing to do with the child's reality, or "So now you know how I feel," which uses the child's experience to vindicate the adult.

This response may be especially tempting when your child's feelings are hard to understand because of differences in your preferences, abilities and experiences, or when they bring up your own issues. (A mother once told me that she responded to her daughter's complaints of a headache by taking two aspirin herself!) Yet responses that confuse your feelings and experiences with those of your child are extremely distracting and can be downright mean-spirited. This response speaks to the need for a sense of separateness, as well as the ability to get at least one step beyond one's own reality.

FIXING THE PROBLEM

The last set of nonsupportive responses are those that attempt to "fix it" or make it better. You'll use these responses when you want to comfort a child or change the situation that's creating the feelings. These responses are triggered by the little voice in our heads that frantically yells, *"Do something!"* — the part of us that hears an expression of feelings as a call to rescue or help.

These responses are especially tempting because, for one thing, they enhance our need to feel useful and important and, for another, they *seem* supportive and are usually done with the best intentions. But as well-intended as they may be, these responses invariably interfere with the child's ability to process feelings and solve problems because they take the responsibility for both out of the child's hands.

Advising

Many adults see their role in their relationships with children as one of advisor. After all, we have experience, knowledge and perspective to justify this role. But is advice-giving the response that's called for? For example, there's a difference between "Mom, which blouse goes better with this skirt?" and "I'm scared about that biology test tomorrow!" When you help your child put an outfit together, you're responding to a request for instruction and information. When you respond to the child's test anxiety with advice to "Just get upstairs and study!" you are not only disregarding her feelings, you're also communicating an assumption that she's too stupid to figure out what to do.

Advice-giving robs children of valuable opportunities to solve their own problems, as well as the power and confidence that come from figuring things out on their own. Rarely, if ever, is an expression of feelings a cry for advice. So if your kid is upset that he can't get a date for the prom, can you simply *hear* his disappointment, anger, frustration or sadness without telling him to get his hair cut, lose five pounds or try calling his cousin Lucy again?

Rescuing

Another interfering technique is called rescuing, which involves solving children's problems for them in order to relieve them of their feelings: "How 'bout if I call my friends and see if any of their daughters are free on prom night?"; "That's okay, son, I'll go have a talk with that teacher" or "Here, let me see those math problems." Rescuing communicates that somehow the child's feelings and problems are also *your* feelings and problems and, like advising, it suggests that the child is incapable of dealing with either of these on his own.

Commiserating

Finally, there's commiserating. "Ain't it awful"; "He's a jerk" or "Well, you don't need her anyway" may sound supportive, but this approach tends to reinforce victim behavior and self-righteousness. In certain cases it may even backfire by inviting the child to defend the "jerk's" behavior. Commiserating takes responsibility away from the child because it suggests that the feelings and problems are someone else's fault.

SUPPORTIVE ALTERNATIVES

We're probably all pretty good at *not* supporting our kids. In fact, it may seem as though everything we've learned is harmful. Considering the fact that few of us have had healthy models of supportiveness in our lives, that isn't very surprising. In fact, people are often dismayed — and even feel abandoned — when the person they share their feelings with *doesn't* react with the previous responses. So then, what are more supportive alternatives?

When offering support, less is more — most notably, less talking and less doing. Your role is actually fairly simple: listen, accept and validate. These supportive behaviors will help you avoid the temptation to judge, own, dismiss, "fix" their feelings or tell them what to do. As simple as a supportive role looks, it can present a huge challenge, particularly because much of what's involved in supportiveness means *not* doing something, which is very different from the nonsupportive types of involvement most of us are used to.

Listening

First, supportiveness means listening because in order to feel safe and supported, kids need to be heard. An invitation to share one's feelings suggests that you're available and open to listening: "Do you want to talk?" If the answer is no, allow them to sit with the problem, work things out in private and come back later if they wish: "I'm here if you want to talk about it" or "Let me know if you change your mind." Not forcing the issue communicates respect for their privacy as well as respect for their ability to figure out what they need. Besides, just knowing you're there is enough sometimes.

The bigger challenge is when they *do* want to talk. Teenagers will invariably have adults in their lives who will talk to them, but few have adults in their lives who will listen. Really listen. If you're one of those who typically responds by *doing*, whether that means fixing, dismissing, distracting, advising or whatever, this role may present a challenge to you as well.

You're probably listening if your mouth isn't doing much. You can't talk and listen at the same time, but by all means acknowledge your children. When you do talk, let them know you hear them and respect what they're saying: "I see"; "I understand" or "I know what you mean." Or just nodding as they talk can be an appropriate and valuable response that invites children to elaborate if they feel the need.

It helps if you can clear your mind — and your agenda — enough to concentrate on what they're saying. If your son wants to talk at a time that isn't convenient for you, tell him, "I want to hear about this. I'm in the middle of something I can't walk away from right now, but I will be able to give you my complete attention in about ten minutes." Or, "Wait a minute. I just got home and I need a few minutes to unwind. Give me till 4:30 and I'll be able to give you the attention you deserve." These boundaries take care of your needs even as they demonstrate your concern and your intention to hear what he has to say.

Choose a time that works for both of you and while your child is talking, stay focused on him. He probably won't feel as if he's really being heard if you spend the entire time he's talking trying to read the paper and repeating "uh-huh" at regular intervals.

Accepting

Accepting is another component of supportiveness. This simply means that you will hear what your kids are saying without making judgments about what they are feeling — even if their feelings are different from the ones you would probably experience in the same situation, even if their feelings don't make much sense to you or even if their feelings trigger surprise or discomfort for you. You don't have to do anything to demonstrate acceptance; your acceptance will be conveyed by the absence of nonaccepting reactions and responses.

Validating

Another ingredient of supportive behavior, validation, will come from anything you say that gives your kids permission to have their feelings. Children may not be looking for answers nearly as much as they're seeking acknowledgment, understanding and the right to be taken seriously.

You can validate by rephrasing what you've heard: "Sounds like you're having a hard time with this" or "You're saying that being singled out was the part that felt unfair to you." You can validate by agreeing: "It hurts to be made fun of when you've made a mistake."

The words "I understand" can be very validating, but remember that teenagers will often believe that *nobody* understands, least of all adults, and especially not their parents. (Sometimes sharing similar experiences can be validating, but more often than not they can simply be distracting. Be careful that you don't keep shifting the focus back to you.) You can validate by just letting the feelings happen without asking for any justification for having them. Remember, supportiveness recognizes that it's okay for children to have feelings without explaining or defending them.

Even if children say something hurtful to you, you can still validate and accept their feelings without getting hooked by what they say. It may be hard not to take "I hate you" rather personally, but the fewer buttons such a statement pushes for you the less likely the child will attempt to continue using it to hurt or manipulate you. You can acknowledge the child's feelings without shaming, getting defensive or hurting back, which will help him feel and work through his anger. For example, "You're really angry with me right now." If you find yourself getting a little hot under the collar, disengage: "Let's talk about this a little later." By saying this and backing away temporarily, you give the child — and yourself — some emotional space.

Supportiveness may come easier when we can recognize that feelings are not behaviors. While feelings are never right or wrong, behaviors that hurt other people are not okay. Adults do not need to protect other people from a child's feelings, but they may need to intervene in hurtful behaviors.

Keep your role — and your separateness — in mind. Remember, you are not responsible for changing or controlling your child's feelings. It's more loving and supportive to communicate that a child's feelings are heard, respected and taken seriously than it is to "fix" the situation, rescue the child from the feelings or try to make the feelings go away. Children learn to deal with feelings more effectively when they don't have to "stuff" or hide them to protect a guilt-ridden or overreacting adult.

Supportiveness may be one of the most valuable tools for relationship building — not just with children, but with anyone in your life. While the old, nonsupportive patterns may be difficult to break, start by noticing which ones you're most tempted to fall back on. Practice listening — with your mouth closed. Let feelings happen without judging or interfering. And watch how these new, supportive responses benefit everyone involved!

Table 25.1 Nonsupportive Responses
To Children's Feelings And Problems

- **Goal:** Make the feelings go away.
- **Purpose:** Protect children from their feelings or protect adults who are uncomfortable with children's feelings.
- **Outcomes:** Children's self-doubt, confusion; need to "stuff" feelings; feelings not okay.

Strategy:	Sounds like:
Dismissing/ Minimizing	"That's nothing to be upset over." "That doesn't mean anything." "So she called you a camel. Big deal!"
Excusing	"She didn't mean it." "He didn't know what he was saying." "She must be having a bad day." "Well, her parents are going through a divorce."
Denying	"Oh, you don't really feel that way." "There's no such thing as monsters." "People shouldn't hate their brothers." "I'm sure your teacher doesn't hate you."
Distracting	"But you're so good in your other subjects." "Things could be worse." "You're lucky you *have* a brother." "You think *you've* got problems." "But his parents are so nice."
Medicating	Uses some type of substance (usually food) or activity (e.g., schoolwork, TV, chores, shopping) to distract children from their feelings.

- **Goal:** Make the child wrong for having feelings.
- **Purpose:** Outlet for adult's anger, impatience, frustration or feelings of inadequacy or shame triggered by child's feelings.
- **Outcome:** Child's sense of shame/wrongness; defensiveness; feelings not okay.

Strategy:	Sounds like:
Attacking/ Shaming	"I *told* you this would happen!" "Don't be a sissy." "You're so ungrateful!"

	"Nice boys don't hate their sisters." "You're just *too* sensitive." "How could you be so stupid?"
Blaming	"What did you do to her?" "Well, if you had just studied!" "Of course it died! You never changed the water!" "That's what happens when you overeat."
Challenging	"Why does that bother you?" (Requires child to defend feelings, convincing adult that the feelings are legitimate/getting adult's approval for feelings)
Enmeshing	"Well *I* never had a problem with math." "So now you know how *I* feel." "Your problems really give me a headache."

- **Goal:** "Fix it"/Make it better.
- **Purpose:** Makes adult responsible for child's problems and allows adult to feel important.
- **Outcome:** Reduced sense of responsibility for problems (for child); lack of confidence in problem-solving abilities; learned helplessness; using feelings to get "rescued."

Strategy:	Sounds like:
Advising	"Go study and you won't feel so scared about that test." "Tell her how you feel." "You know if you cut your hair and lost five pounds, you wouldn't feel that way." "Just ignore her."
Rescuing	"Here, let me see those math problems." "Okay, you can have the car again next weekend if you have a good enough excuse for breaking curfew." "Look, I'll talk to your teacher about it." "That's okay. I'll pay those insurance premiums."
Commiser- ating	"Ain't it awful." "Well, he's a jerk anyway." "You don't need her."

Table 25.2 Supportive Alternatives
For Dealing With Feelings

- Get clear on your role.
- Listen.
- Distinguish between feelings and behaviors.
- Accept the other person's right to have those feelings.
- Validate the other person's experience.
- Maintain your boundaries.
- Leave the door open for future discussions.

EXERCISE

It probably won't be long before you have an opportunity to support your children when they are experiencing feelings. Spend at least ten minutes practicing supportive behaviors (if you can encourage them to talk to you about what's going on). Afterwards, tell how you were able to demonstrate the following:

Supportive listening to your child's feelings.

_____

_____

Acceptance of your child's feelings.

_____

_____

Validation of your child's feelings.

_____

_____

How did your child respond to these supportive behaviors?

_____

_____

In what ways, if any, were these behaviors difficult for you?

Supportive listening to your child's feelings.

_____

_____

Acceptance of your child's feelings.

_____

_____

Validation of your child's feelings.

_____

_____

Which types of nonsupportive responses were you most tempted to use (whether or not you actually used them)?

_____

_____

How might you be even more supportive the next time you have the opportunity to talk with your child?

_____

_____

Twenty-Six

Encourage

Just talking about a troublesome situation can sometimes knock it down to a more solvable size. A supportive environment offers the emotional safety to experience the feelings that go along with the situation which may seem too big or confusing to handle. Acceptance and validation make it easier to process and let go of the feelings. Often this is enough, because sometimes the problem *is* the feelings — the child's reaction to a particular situation — and sometimes the feelings just need a safe place to go. Maybe all your children need is the reassurance that their feelings are okay to have. Once the feelings are expressed, the children can get on with their lives.

There will be times, however, when their feelings suggest problems that require action. Helping children deal with their feelings leaves them free to face the situations that are triggering those feelings. But even then, they may have a hard time finding their way through to a solution.

This is where you come in — but in what capacity? Let's say your son comes home complaining that his teacher hates him. Depending on your child's history and the mood you're in when this happens, you may think to yourself: "Well, gee, maybe if you did your homework and didn't talk in class all the time, she wouldn't pick on you so much." Or "That's ridiculous. Teachers don't hate their students." Or maybe "I'm sure you're overreacting." These thoughts may be more than just old programming — they may be entirely correct, at least from your perspective. But now that you know these responses are neither supportive nor helpful, you'll probably make an effort to avoid verbalizing them. (And, by the way, if comments like these still slip out from time to time, your awareness as well as your commitment to change will eventually make these patterns less likely to continue. It's a process. If you've started noticing your nonsupportive comments sooner, you're making real progress.)

So what *do* you say? Well, you might start by asking for more information: "What's going on?" or "Tell me more." And you'll listen, accepting his reality without judging, minimizing, assigning blame or telling him the way out. The supportive and nonsupportive responses that come up in dealing with your children's feelings also apply here.

You'll also want to validate the child's experience (regardless of how you feel about it): "Hmm. You do have a problem"; "You really feel picked on in this class" or "You're saying it's a personality clash."

Perhaps the greatest challenge for you will be to watch your child struggle with a problem without jumping in with advice or a solution because, very often, the solution will be painfully obvious to you.

UNHELPFUL HELPING

But as tempting as it is, there are some problems with "helping" in this way. Telling your child what he needs to do may indeed lead him to behaviors that will work a lot better. But at what cost? You may have saved him additional grief with this particular teacher, helped him pass a class or keep his grades up, given him words to use to

stick up for himself or brought him a little closer to gra-
duation. These are all worthwhile goals, but they are really beside the point. Because in *giving* your child a solution
you've also robbed him of an opportunity to take responsibility for solving a problem on his own, and this is a skill
he'll need long after this teacher has ceased to be a part of
his life.

There are other problems with advice-giving. One is
the "yeah but" syndrome, in which no matter what you
suggest, your child will tell you why it won't work. After
three or four "yeah buts," you'll probably be out of ideas
and feeling rather frustrated and resentful that your child
isn't listening to you. As a result, you'll probably slip
right back into such negative responses as shaming and
blaming.

Another problem with advice-giving is that it's usually
based on *your* needs, reality and value system. What might
be best for you — and possibly much of the rest of the
world — may not necessarily be best for your child. What
if, God forbid, your advice is wrong? What if it's misinter-
preted or carried out incorrectly? What if it creates additional problems for the child? Guess who gets the blame?

One more thing: Advice-giving actually disempowers
and creates dependence. Somewhere down the line, your
kids are going to run into challenges that require quick
thinking, processing and decision-making, and you're not
going to be there to tell them what to do. What then?
This is another boundary issue, one that concerns the
ownership of a problem and the responsibility for its solution. If your son is having a conflict with one of his
teachers, are you able to see this as his problem and not
yours? Without this boundary, you are always going to
find yourself in the middle of things for which your child
needs to assume responsibility.

If you're used to playing the role of advisor, you're
probably going to feel like you're abandoning this poor
person in his hour of need. Not so. You're just switching
the role you play in this part of your child's life. Although

you don't allow his problems to become your problems, you are still very much "there." But instead of fixing, rescuing or advising, you become a guide, an encourager, someone who facilitates your child's exploration and discovery — not only of his needs in this situation, but also of the dimensions of the problem, the options he has available to him and the possible outcomes of trying these options. Even when kids come to you for advice, wanting you to tell them what they should do, your task is to steer them back to finding a solution on their own.

You'll do this by asking instead of telling. In other words, when your son says, "My teacher hates me"; "I want to break up with my girlfriend"; "I'm tired of never having enough money" or "I think I'm flunking Spanish," your response will come in the form of a question. These questions will vary from one situation to another, but they will essentially encourage your child to explore his options: "What do you want to happen (or accomplish)?"; "What do you plan to do about that?"; "Have you tried that before?"; "How has that worked for you?"; "What do you think will happen if you do that?"; "How do you think you'll feel after that?"; "What other options do you have?"; "Can you live with that?"

Specific questions with regard to our example might be: "What does this teacher seem to want?"; "How would you like her to treat you?"; "What have you tried that's worked in the past?"; "How badly do you want to pass this class?"; "What are you willing to do differently?"; "How do you think she'll feel about that?"; "What if that doesn't work?"; "What else can you do?"

Ask — don't tell. Your questions reflect, support and encourage, while keeping the responsibility for the problem's solution with the child.

Listen and accept, no matter what your children suggest. Some of their answers may not be what you wanted to hear because they're still testing the limits of your trust (and their safety), because they're still in the middle of their feelings or because what they're proposing actually seems like a good idea to them at the moment. When your son proposes dropping out of school or putting a contract out on the teacher, your ultimate challenge may be to stay cool and even validate the fact that it would certainly eliminate the problem. So if he's trying to shock and you don't act shocked, he will probably move on to a solution that's a little less drastic. The same may be true if he's just letting off steam.

SOLUTIONS WITHOUT HARM

Naturally we get a little nervous about seemingly destructive responses from our kids because we sometimes confuse desires with actions. In this case you can be supportive by helping him distinguish between the two. For example, wanting to drop out of school is a desire which, like a feeling, is exempt from judgment. It's okay to *want* to do this, especially under the circumstances. In fact, validating the desire ("I know you wish you could just walk away from it all right now.") may be all the kid needs before he can let go and consider another more constructive course of action. Rarely are there any negative consequences from simply wanting to do something, especially when he's given "permission" to have that desire. If he doesn't have to defend or obsess about the desire (because of a lack of power, support and more positive alternatives), he can make room for other ideas.

On the other hand, actually dropping out is an action with consequences probably even more uncomfortable than the original conflict. If you can keep a cool head, your questions can help your child weigh the consequences of one course of action against another and make his choices accordingly.

If your children propose solutions that can hurt other people, they are probably still feeling a lot of anger and frustration. While the ideas themselves are not necessarily destructive, actions that are inspired by anger and frustration can indeed be destructive. (Even telling the teacher that you hate her is a verbal attack that violates her rights and self-esteem.)

This brings up another point: Not only do we need to encourage children to distinguish between feelings (which are okay) and actions (which sometimes are not okay), we also need to help them learn how to express feelings without violating anyone else. This part will be easier if you started with your children when they were young because as they get older, their ability to hurt only increases. However, even if it feels as if it's too late, it probably isn't.

If your child is extremely upset, help him deal with the feelings before encouraging him to work on a solution. The process of brainstorming, evaluating and predicting outcomes is a fairly rational process that will go more smoothly once your kids get to externalize their feelings. Acknowledge your child's anger and, if nothing else, give him a little time and space to cool down.

You might also want to suggest that he do something to release the anger, like punching pillows, yelling and throwing a tantrum on the bed, writing a letter to the person he's angry with and then tearing it into 100 pieces, drawing a picture of how he's feeling or what he wishes he could do, throwing pebbles into a pond or at a tree in a field, going for a brisk walk or writing in a journal. Let him suggest a strategy that will work for him. As long as it doesn't harm the furniture, plants, pets, other people or himself, any strategy your kid uses to unload angry feelings is better than stuffing them in. Afterwards, he may be ready for some constructive problem-solving.

THE "I DON'T KNOW" ANSWERS

One of the most frustrating experiences you may encounter in this process is a series of "I-don't-know" answers. Your child may not know for a number of reasons, not the least of which is actually not knowing. If she's in the middle of a lot of feelings, if she's more likely to complain than she is to actually take responsibility for her problems or if she tends to solve problems rather impulsively, she probably hasn't given a lot of thought to some of the issues you've raised. She may just need a little time: "Why don't you think about it for a while? Let's talk about it later."

"I don't know" can be a very handy response. In addition to buying your child a little time, it can also get her a lot of attention. "I don't know" can help her avoid assuming responsibility for the problem. It may even get an exasperated parent to just do it for her: "Oh all right! I'll go talk to him."

HELP WITHOUT PROVIDING SOLUTIONS

Even if your children have learned that acting helpless invariably results in someone taking over and smoothing things out for them, they can eventually learn to take responsibility for their own solutions when other people quit playing along. Backing out by offering them a little time to think things through — rather than jumping in with advice or, worse yet, solving the problem for them — will gently and lovingly push the problem back in their laps, where it belongs.

If kids are really invested in solving the problem — and not just talking about it to get attention, a reaction or a rescue — they may be willing to take some time to think about it or even write about it (which, incidentally, is a great way to sort through problems). Go back at a later time and ask your child: "What did you decide to do about the situation with your teacher?"

In the course of your discussions, it's appropriate to ask, "How can I help you?" or "What would you like from me?" as long as you stay clear on your role. Be assured that children may, especially at first, see these questions as invitations to ask you to call the school to get them out of a test, write their thank-you notes for them or double their allowance. You can still hear their ideas without making judgments, although occasionally you may need to respond with a boundary such as, "No, that wouldn't work for me"; "I wouldn't be comfortable doing that" or "It isn't my place to do that."

Encourage them to make other suggestions that you can, indeed, live with: check their answers on study papers, provide them with stationery, loan them your good pen or find extra jobs they can do around the house for extra money. In this way you are providing support and encouragement without providing solutions for them.

When the dust settles, ask your child some follow-up questions, such as: "How did that situation work out?"; "How do you feel about what happened?"; "How do you think you'll handle this next time?"; "What will you do differently the next time it happens?" or "What can you do to avoid this problem in the future?"

Children experience a great deal of power in solving their own problems and in knowing that something is working better because of some decision they've made. There is much confidence to be gained from this power, which will serve your children well when they are faced with decisions to be made in the absence of an adult's advice or supervision (which will often be when the stakes are the highest). In the end, their track record will be built not on your advice, warnings or admonitions, but on the support and encouragement you've offered them along the way.

EXERCISE

Identify a problem your child is having that you would be willing (and welcome) to help find a solution for.

_____

_____

_____

In talking to your child about this problem, identify questions you might ask to help find a solution.

_____

_____

_____

In addition to listening, accepting, validating your child's feelings and experiences, and asking the previous questions, in what other ways would you be willing to support and encourage? (Be careful that you do not end up taking responsibility for the problem or its solution.)

_____

_____

_____

Twenty-seven

Trust

Healthy relationships require trust on many levels. With children this can be especially tough because many things can interfere with trust, especially if they have a history that includes anything from habitually poor judgment to pathological lying.

The challenge is amplified by the fact that, unlike love and acceptance, trust is conditional and needs to be earned. You may trust unconditionally that your daughter is capable of wisdom, insight and responsible choice, but her actual behavior may have repeatedly demonstrated otherwise. How can you restructure your relationship to leave space for that to change? The goal here is not to trust blindly or to deny prior trust violations. Instead, the goal is to give your children new opportunities to earn your trust until they succeed. This requires a sense of unconditional trust in the learning process as well as in the process of building healthy and loving relationships.

The process of rebuilding trust involves setting boundaries and following through on contingencies specified in the boundaries. Let's say your child has compromised a privilege by breaking an agreement. For example, you've agreed to let your child use your stereo but only under certain conditions. Somewhere down the line she used a piece of equipment that she'd agreed was off limits, forgot to put a dozen CDs back in their cases or cranked up the volume to a level that blew out the speakers (or windows). Do you react by putting the stereo in a vault until she turns 30? Since that won't teach her how to use it responsibly and will put you in a position of having to go without music for a few years, banning the stereo will probably not be your first choice, even if it is your first impulse. But how can you ever trust her with the stereo again?

Believe it or not, breaches such as these are wonderful opportunities for your children to learn, grow and assume responsibility for their behavior. But these errors become learning opportunities only when handled as a boundary violation (instead of a personal attack or a character disorder) with consistent and immediate follow through.

Obviously your child isn't ready to handle this responsibility yet. If equipment was damaged, she is responsible for repairs (so long as the damage was the result of a boundary violation and not something you forgot to demonstrate or require as a condition of the equipment's use). Will she pay for fixing or replacing damaged equipment from her savings, allowance or job earnings? Will she work it off with additional responsibilities around the house or does she have another acceptable plan to cover these expenses? Are you willing to hold her to this commitment even though it may take months?

Whether or not anything was broken, it may be necessary to set a new boundary. Rather than attacking your daughter, attack the problem: "This isn't working. We need to renegotiate these arrangements." This may translate into asking her to play only her own tapes or CDs, to use the stereo only when you're home or to give the equipment a "rest" for a little while. For example, "Let's try again in a month (or after you've replaced the CD you broke or after you've come up with a plan to use this stereo as we had agreed)."

REGAINING TRUST

You are asking her how she's going to do things differently next time. In this way you're leaving the door open for her to try again — and get it right this time — but only after expenses for damaged equipment have been paid or reimbursed, and only after she's made a new commitment in the form of a plan that demonstrates how she's going to use the stereo within the boundaries you've set. If, instead of a plan, she solves the problem by saving up and buying her own stereo, that's fine (although she still owes you for anything of yours that needed to replace or repaired). She doesn't need a plan. She's solved the problem and your stereo is safe.

Even if you're beginning with very little trust, you can express your desire to start over: "I understand we've had problems in the past. I've had a hard time trusting you because of all the times that trust has been violated. I am trying to change many things in this relationship and I'm willing to start from scratch on this one. I really want to trust you and I believe you are capable of acting in trustworthy ways. I will need some evidence, though, and a commitment from you that demonstrates I can trust you."

One mother asked her children to tell her three areas in which they wanted to be trusted and used their suggestions as a basis for negotiations. She selected an area for each child that allowed for clear and specific boundaries, that required the fewest concessions from her and that posed the smallest threat to her possessions or her children's safety. As the power dynamics began shifting, and the trust between her and her children was slowly reestablished, this mother was able to offer looser boundaries with fewer restrictions, more privileges and greater responsibility.

Problem of Friends

You may find yourself saying, "I *do* trust my children. It's the people they hang around with that I don't trust." This statement still reflects a lack of trust because it suggests that you don't trust your children to set boundaries to take care of themselves in their relationships with their friends.

It may be very difficult to accept that your child's friends did not *make* him break curfew, flunk geometry, "get high," have sex, cut school or start smoking. This is about your child's inability or unwillingness to say no. (In fact, it may even have been your child's idea in the first place.) "Bad influences" can be a convenient excuse, and such influences will always exist. But holding children accountable for their behavior regardless of the influences in their lives — and not blaming them, making excuses for them or allowing them to blame their friends — eventually will help them become less vulnerable to those influences.

This is why trust is so important. Throughout their lives, your children will meet, befriend, date and even marry people you might not trust. If you try to control your children's relationships, they're likely to resist, spending their energies defending these relationships rather then evaluating them. In a win-lose power struggle especially, your objections are only going to make the person you're objecting to more attractive to your kids. Avoid any investment in making your kids — or their choices — wrong, but leave the door open for them to figure out on their own that a relationship with a certain person may not be the best choice for a friend (or for the person to surprise you by turning out to be okay).

Another strategy for building trust in relationships is modeling trustworthy behavior yourself. If your children have had reason to mistrust you, are you willing to acknowledge past violations, make the necessary reparations and amends and — most important — change your behavior? (Simply apologizing while doing the same things over and over wears thin fairly quickly.) The more consistently your children see you following through on your commitments, living up to standards you hold for them and taking responsibility for your feelings and behaviors, the more comfortable they may be with letting down their guard and maybe even imitating what you're doing.

If your trust issues are based on a long history of aggressive behavior, lying and rebellion, it is still possible to restore trust to the relationship, although it may take a little longer. Continual defiance and rule-breaking are usually symptoms of unbalanced power dynamics more than they are simple trust issues. Sometimes simply re-structuring these dynamics — in the way you respond to your children's behavior and needs, in the way you ask for cooperation and in the way you and your teen come to agreements — can eliminate the need for defiance. In the meantime, you might have to put your valuables in storage or even, in extreme instances, change the locks on your doors. But if you've been attempting even a few of the ideas in the previous chapters, you probably won't have to go to such radical ends to take care of yourself and your household. And it may not take as long as you might imagine.

EXERCISE

Describe an area where your trust in your child is weaker than either of you might like.

_____

_____

What events or experiences have contributed to this lack of trust?

_____

_____

What type of commitment and/or behavior would it take for you to be able to trust your child again in a similar situation?

_____

_____

What are you willing to do or offer in order to give your child another opportunity to regain your trust?

_____

_____

Under what circumstances would you be willing to do or offer what you described above?

_____

_____

In what areas might your child mistrust you?

_____

_____

What are you willing to do to regain your child's trust?

_____

_____

Detach

If things get ugly, if you start to lose your cool, if someone's comments or criticisms trigger a shame attack or if your child's behavior sends you into an emotional tailspin, it's time to detach. Detachment means disconnecting — from the event, the experience, the craziness, the person or the results of someone else's decisions and behaviors. It does not mean abandoning; it's closer to letting go.

Detaching means setting boundaries between your feelings and someone else's. It is a very basic skill in taking care of yourself in any relationship. Detaching allows you to stop explaining and defending yourself to earn someone's approval (or minimize their disapproval). It allows you to avoid changing your behavior, making a big deal about things you really don't care about or compromising your integrity to achieve the same goals.

Detaching allows you to extricate yourself from invasive or abusive situations without requiring you to either take revenge or pretend to be "fine." It entitles others to their feelings — including their disapproval and judgments — although it doesn't require that you change, participate in, be responsible for or even know about those feelings. It even enables you to love unconditionally and accept someone whose behaviors may be so toxic that an actual relationship is impossible.

Ideally we'd all like to stay calm and serene in the face of the most extreme situation. If you can pull this off, more power to you. If not, there are a few techniques that can help you disengage, even in not-so-extreme situations — those that feel just a bit uncomfortable.

Let's say, for example, that you and your kids have come to an agreement about how they keep their rooms. Their messes are confined to their own space and don't create problems for anyone else in the household. Yet your mother (in-laws, neighbors or anyone in your life who is capable of pushing your buttons) simply can't believe you'd allow such chaos to exist. What happens when this person criticizes the way you parent?

One father explained that he finally stopped trying to defend his behavior when he realized that no explanation would ever convince his mother-in-law that any way other than her way was acceptable: "I simply tell her, 'It works for us' and start talking about something else."

Another parent said she was able to defuse a potential conflict by simply agreeing: "Yeah, really" or "No kidding." Then she, too, changed the subject. Another found "Thank you for sharing that" does the trick for her. Another uses "We don't need to discuss that" or "I don't care to talk about that."

And another parent, whose sister was in the habit of letting her know exactly what everybody else in the family thought of her parenting skills, finally came back with, "That's none of my business," and moved on to other matters.

SETTING BOUNDARIES

The point of these statements — and the immediate switch to another topic — is to set a boundary by gently and firmly making it clear that the subject is not open for discussion. In this way, you refuse to participate in trying to get someone to understand and approve because neither their understanding nor their approval is relevant to the situation. No one needs to okay your parenting goals or actions. Even if something isn't working for you, you are not obligated to listen to someone else's advice or criticism. These boundaries allow you to screen out information you really don't need to hear.

Other People

The same holds true whenever people try to get to your children through you. Being in the middle never helped anybody. Detaching gives you a way out. For example, when your mother complains that her grandchildren haven't written her any thank-you notes for the gifts she gave them last Christmas, is she simply expressing a frustration or asking you to intervene on her behalf? You can support her frustration without taking responsibility for "getting" the kids to write to her in much the same way you encourage a child to solve a problem without doing it for him. If she's upset that they haven't responded, doesn't she need to talk to *them* instead of you? Can you support her right to work it out with them, to discontinue gift-giving until they are willing to acknowledge what they receive or to handle it in whatever way she sees fit?

Your Partner

If you have a parenting partner, the same goes for him or her. Many of us grew up in homes in which one parent — usually the mother — put a lot of energy into "protecting" the other parent from the kids' messes, problems, needs and noise. In healthy families, individuals take responsibility for creating their own boundaries without requiring an intermediary, caring and consideration notwithstanding.

School

The same is also true in schools, which have a longstanding tradition of letting parents in on problems between teachers and students, hoping that the parents will correct the situation. If a teacher calls you simply to let you know that something is going on, that's one thing. But what if the teacher sees you as an ally in his efforts to "get" the kid when she messes up?

Again, detaching will allow you to overcome old people-pleasing issues that come up when the school calls. Often the image of the "good parent" collapses with a call about a problem in which the child's failure becomes the parent's failure. Detaching will help ward off the feelings of shame and frustration that can trigger whatever reaction you might consider in an attempt to reinstate an image of parental control and competence. This isn't about your parenting. This is between your child and the school.

You can stay out of the middle by asking for details about the incident, about the school's policy and about what the teacher has tried or will try to do. You might also ask why you've been called. If your intervention is solicited, you can refuse to be put in a position of exacting a confession or punishing your child for something you did not see. Your role in these instances is to allow the school's consequences to occur (as much as you may hate to see your child sit in detention, lose grade points or miss the game on Saturday) and to help your child decide how she's going to make more positive choices in the future.

ABUSIVE SITUATIONS

Of all the times you'll need to detach, none will be more essential than when you are engaged in an interaction with someone who becomes either verbally or physically abusive. As you renegotiate the terms of your relationship with your kids, chances are you and your children will be less likely to push one another quite as close to the edge. There is no place for abuse in healthy interactions; however, even healthy people can have unhealthy moments. Even with the best intentions, any of us can blow it in the heat of the moment. If abusive behavior appears to have worked for you in the past, you may find these patterns difficult to resist. The same goes for your children, especially if you've frequently allowed yourself to be the victim of their abuse, or if you have had a habit of excusing, denying or allowing their abusive behavior.

Even arguing requires boundaries. Remember, we want to support one another's angry feelings, but when angry feelings are expressed as hurtful behaviors — such as yelling, name-calling, insults, put-downs or any form of angry physical contact — it's time for a loud cry of, "Stop!" Short and sweet, this boundary lets your child know he's crossed the line, especially if you follow with another boundary that lets him know: "I'll continue this discussion when you can talk to me without yelling." Then you walk away. Go into another room. Shut the door if you need to (but try not to slam it). Leave the house if you need to. Stop participating, absolutely and immediately. But, as always, leave open the possibility to pick up where you left off before things got too hot, but only when you're *both* ready.

You will have some feelings of your own from all of this. Give yourself time to calm down. If your kid wants to talk — without yelling — and you're still trying to get your blood pressure down, let him know: "I'm not ready yet. I need a while to cool off." You're not going to be much good to anyone until you catch your breath and let go of some of your own anger. Later, you may be able to be part of a civilized discussion without doing much formal emotional processing, but at some point you will probably want to deal with whatever this exchange has brought up for you.

Eventually, you may not even end up getting as upset about things as you used to because detaching allows you to depersonalize conflicts to a large extent. You'll see a messy counter as just a messy counter: ("These counters are a mess.") instead of an indication of a flawed child ("You are such an inconsiderate slob!"). In the long run, it will enhance your relationships, protect your kids and, most of all, reduce a great number of stresses in your life.

Detachment can be a long and tedious journey in a world that's taught us to react, control and even take changes in the weather rather personally. However, it's a journey that's worth every step.

EXERCISE

In the past, which patterns or messages have been obstacles in your ability to detach?

_____

_____

Describe an incident in the past that probably would have been less stressful for all concerned if you had detached.

_____

_____

- If you had it to do over again, at what point would you detach?

  _____

  _____

- How would you detach?

  _____

  _____

- Under what conditions would you resume contact?

  _____

  _____

- In what way might the situation have turned out differently if you had detached?

  _____

  _____

Identify at least three other situations you can anticipate in which you may have to detach.

1. _____

2. _____

3. _____

Why will you want to detach in each of these situations?

1. _____

2. _____

3. _____

How will you detach in each of these situations?

1. _____

2. _____

3. _____

Twenty-nine

Self-Care

I'll never forget the first time I heard a flight attendant give that little speech about putting on an oxygen mask in the event of a loss of cabin pressure. She was advising passengers traveling with children to put on their own masks first and then assist the children. I was positive that she had it backwards. "She's new," I thought.

I've probably heard that speech a thousand times since then and it never fails to strike me as odd. Although I've certainly spoken and written enough about it, and may even understand it on an intellectual level, the idea of taking care of yourself first, *so you'll be more useful to the people around you,* is still a fairly novel concept to me.

Of all the ingredients of healthy relationships, the most important by far is our ability to take care of ourselves. Naturally the quality of the care we can give others is going to be affected by the shape we're in. Although I hope I never need to find out, I imagine it would be far easier to help another person put on his oxygen mask if I were actually breathing myself. In terms of our relationships, the same principle applies: *We can't give what we don't have.*

For example, it's easier to love another person in healthy ways when we can love ourselves first. Likewise, we need a certain degree of physical and emotional well-being to nurture the same in another person. We can even listen to another person more patiently and attentively when we've taken a few minutes to collect our own thoughts.

DON'T LET THE WELL RUN DRY

In a culture that often equates giving with goodness, we can easily forget to tend the well so that it doesn't run dry. Unfortunately, we're just not going to be much use to anyone unless we occasionally restock our supply of physical vitality, mental clarity, emotional equilibrium, positivity and self-esteem. If our own needs continue to go unmet, the type of support we are able to offer will be marginal at best.

Plus, we're better able to model the behavior we want our children to adopt when we're taking care of ourselves. How can we teach children to ask for what they need, stick up for themselves and disengage from destructive and abusive interactions if we don't practice these self-caring behaviors ourselves?

Relationship Building

Self-care is an essential ingredient for building healthy relationships because we're less likely to exhibit hurtful, passive-aggressive or self-destructive tendencies in relationships when we've done what was needed to take care of ourselves.

If you've read this far, you're probably not the kind of person who sits around every day dreaming of ways to blow your children's minds. I honestly believe that the vast majority of parents do not harm their children intentionally. And yet we're vulnerable to attitudes, behaviors and patterns in our language that can indeed hurt children. Even when we know better, it can be easy to cross that line.

Usually we do hurtful things to kids for one of three reasons. Sometimes it's just a matter of bad habits, patterns that go unquestioned because they are so familiar and pervasive. We say or do things without thinking. Or we even do things deliberately, with the best intentions — such as advice-giving or rescuing — that seem helpful but, in the long run, do more harm than good.

Sometimes we've neglected to set a boundary. For example, we try to take a few minutes for ourselves after a rough day at work, but that's when our kids ambush us with their needs. We get overstressed and forget to notice. We've had something come up with the boss, the spouse, a neighbor, our parents or maybe even the car that we haven't yet had a chance to work through. The kid gets the brunt of it, sometimes just for being in the wrong place at the wrong time.

But even more often, hurtful behaviors come from unresolved issues from our own childhood experiences, times we were hurt or damaging messages we've received. These issues may emerge in our own behaviors as one of the following:

- A fear of conflict
- A need for approval
- Discomfort around someone else's feelings
- A need to look good
- A need to be in control
- A distorted sense of responsibility for someone else's feelings and behaviors
- A need to be needed
- A lack of personal boundaries (or a lack of respect for another person's boundaries)
- Actual parenting behaviors that can range from neglect to true cruelty.

Until we clean up these old hurts, the choices we have about the way we interact with our own kids will be very limited, no matter what our intentions.

So the first challenge in talking about self-care is shifting the focus from the outside to the inside. Many of us are experts at identifying and anticipating other people's needs and feelings, yet we are overwhelmed when faced with the task of figuring out our own. This gets easier as we break old patterns in which we defined ourselves by other people's needs, feelings and reactions to us. At times it may actually mean stopping — often in mid-conflict — to ask ourselves questions such as, "What's going on here?" "What am I feeling?" or "What do I need right now?"

It may be necessary to stop a discussion or put down what you're doing to focus on what's going on inside. If the situation doesn't get clear right away — and often it won't — you may need to sit with a feeling, talk with someone who isn't immediately involved or write about what's going on to get a better sense of how you can take care of yourself. Whether you need to spend a few minutes alone to "come down" from your day, set or renegotiate a boundary, stop what you're doing and get involved in a different activity or walk away from a fight (or even a relationship), your efforts to take focused, effective and appropriate self-caring actions require you to figure out what you need.

This will help you with another self-caring behavior: asking for what you want. The better sense we have of our needs in any given situation, the better we can communicate those needs and have them met. Yet many of us have been conditioned not to speak up for ourselves, thinking it selfish, knowing that it puts us at risk of being rejected, ridiculed or ignored. It's true that we may not always get what we ask for (and asking may ignite some conflict we'd rather not have to deal with) but, we certainly increase the odds of getting what we want when we do. And we also reduce the chances of feeling resentment or acting out when the people around us can't figure out on their own what we need.

TRUST

Self-care requires trusting others to be able to take care of themselves. It also requires being able to let go enough to allow them to do so without taking it personally when they don't do it exactly the way you'd like. This may mean having the courage to ask for a hug or invite someone to go see a movie with the understanding that it's okay for them to say no. It also means that if a person isn't able to give you what you ask for, you have some other recourse to get your needs met, either by waiting until that person is available, seeking another person to give you support or finding some activity you are willing to do on your own.

Self-care also means trusting that other people will eventually manage even if you turn them down or withdraw from an interaction that is uncomfortable for you. In this regard, self-care means you don't have to coddle or protect people when you don't want to do something with or for them. You can indeed just say no without offering excuses or explanations. Or you can communicate what you are willing to do, when you'll be available or under what conditions you will accommodate their needs. In other words, you can set boundaries. If necessary, you can let them get angry or act hurt without reacting, defending or even participating.

SUPPORT SYSTEM

Self-care often requires a support system: people who will accept you in whatever shape you're in and encourage you to make self-caring decisions. If most of the people in your life have encouraged you to sacrifice or abandon yourself, believing that was necessary in order to take care of them or make them look good, they probably will not be a part of your support network, at least in the beginning. Look instead for positive, healthy people who won't feel threatened by your self-caring behaviors; people who will listen without judging or advising and people who will respect your needs and validate your reality.

If your family or friends don't have these supportive behaviors to offer you, help them learn and practice them by asking for them. A friend once told me that the first time she ever got sick, she actually had to explain to her husband that she needed for him to give her soup, put his arm around her shoulder and say, "Poor baby" a few times. He'd never received much support, sympathy or even soup from his family when he was sick and figured he was being helpful by just staying out of her way.

Most of us grow up without a clue as to what supportive behavior is, so be specific: "I'm having a hard time. I need someone to listen to me and let me cry. It will help if you can hold me and just let me know you understand. Don't say anything else, okay?" In dealing with your kids, you may need to ask for support in the form of time to yourself, a half hour without the stereo or TV, some specific feedback, their attention, an agreement to discuss a problem without getting personal, some form of cooperation or an acknowledgment that they've heard and understood something you've said. You may be surprised at how quickly people can learn to be supportive when you ask for what you need, especially if you've been modeling these behaviors when the shoe's been on the other foot.

Even if your family is willing and able to be there for you, there will be times when you'll want support from someone outside the family. This is particularly true if you begin dealing with your own addictions or compulsive behaviors, unresolved childhood issues or current patterns or conflicts that involve people in your family. In these instances, a counselor or therapist, a support group or some healthy, supportive friends (with good boundaries of their own) can help you get through the tight spots.

Even if we've been encouraged to "tough it out", we know that it is very destructive to keep our issues secret in order to protect the people around us. Self-care recognizes the need for interdependency, at least occasionally. It means believing that you deserve to have someone be there for you, that it's okay to reach out, that there's no shame in needing someone to lean on from time to time, that you don't need to do it alone.

As you incorporate these behaviors and beliefs into your life, you may notice a significant increase in the supportive people you begin to attract. As your boundaries get clearer and as your convictions to healthy, supportive relationships grow, you'll find either that abusive people are no longer quite as present in your life or, if they are, they are no longer behaving quite as abusively. This is a nice change.

By the same token, if in the past you've been the abuser, as you learn to set better boundaries and take better care of yourself, you'll find that you don't need to resort to extreme behavior to get what you need. You won't have the number of resentments you may once have experienced. Many of the "triggers" will have been eliminated. Also, the foundation of mutual respect you've been building will make abusive behavior — or any violation of another person's dignity, safety or worth — increasingly inconceivable.

Will you still get angry? Of course. But instead of stuffing it or hurting someone with it, you now can take responsiblity for your anger and employ healthy, nonhurtful ways of getting it out of your system. For one thing, you won't blame your feelings on others. Even if it seems crystal clear that "I wouldn't be feeling like this if they weren't acting this way," you will recognize that they didn't make your feelings. If you're feeling hurt because your kids scream and say they hate you, you really don't want to say, "When you do that, I feel hurt," even if you do, in fact, react that way. Because that statement not only suggests that your children are responsible for your feelings, but it also implies that being hurt is the only reaction possible for you. If their intention was to hurt, this statement only reinforces their behavior.

You have two issues going on here. One is the need to disengage from a hurtful or uncomfortable situation, which you can do by setting a boundary: "Let's try this a little later without the screaming." You can even validate their feelings first: "You seem really angry right now. Let's talk about this a little later when you can talk without screaming at me."

The second issue is the fact that being screamed at — and hearing "I hate you" from your kids — may sometimes bring up all kinds of feelings, *none of which have anything to do with your children.* That's right. Whatever feelings their words may have triggered come from your needs and your issues. (This also applies to seemingly positive statements like, "When you get good grades, I feel so happy!")

We've been well conditioned to the idea that our feelings — good and bad — are somebody else's fault. While people and events may seem to provoke our feelings, the way we react is influenced by the beliefs we have about ourselves. For example, the more confident we feel about our appearance, our parenting skills or our worth as a human being, the less likely we are to be affected negatively by criticism or disparaging remarks. On the other hand, if we have a lot of unresolved shame issues, feelings of self-doubt and low self-esteem, even a casual glance from a total stranger becomes suspect.

FIND OTHER WAYS TO REACT

There are always other ways to react. Perhaps one day your kids will scream, "I hate you!" and instead of feeling attacked, abandoned and inadequate, you may be surprised, amused or curious. Perhaps you'll just look at them and think, "Boy, they're really having a hard time with this. I'll bet they do hate me now." And beyond that, you won't give it much thought.

But what if, for whatever reasons, you do take it personally? Do you tell your children that they've triggered every unresolved childhood experience you've ever had? Even if they had incredibly strong boundaries and degrees in psychiatry, that would be quite a lot to dump on them. But this doesn't mean pretending that you're fine when you're not, either.

So what do you do with your fears, your sadness and your anger? You may need to say, "Whoa! I'm getting really angry. I need a little time to myself to work through this one. We'll talk later." This is another way of disengaging that does not apply old shame-and-blame tactics for something you're feeling.

Then you tap into your support network, calling or visiting someone with whom you can be angry, crazy, depressed or irrational, and where you can have, express and work through your feelings.

Perhaps you write about what's going on and what's coming up. Or you go for a walk to disengage from your physical environment and get your energy moving in other directions. Or you go to your room or some other safe place where you can have a good cry, pound on a few pillows, tear up a phone book or two or maybe just catch your breath.

You may need to set other boundaries or establish other ground rules for arguing. You may need to find other strategies for sticking to the issues and negotiating solutions. You may need very limited contact for a while. You may even need mediation. But once you've dealt with your feelings, you're likely to be able to deal with the problem from a healthier and more productive perspective. Besides, bear in mind that as your relationships get stronger, as they operate more and more from a foundation of win-win and mutual respect, you're far less likely to encounter angry, contemptuous behavior.

SELF-CARE ISSUES

Self-Forgive

This leads to two other self-care issues. The first is the ability to *self-forgive*. If you're less than thrilled with your track record as a parent, it may help to remember that whether your parenting evolved from the way you were parented, social support for ultimately hurtful behaviors or lack of information, you certainly came by your patterns honestly. No one, including you, will benefit from any shame or self-hatred you may feel. In fact, the sooner you can accept that whatever you did was the best you could do at the time, the sooner you can move on to more loving and self-caring behaviors. *We cannot change the past, but we can allow the past to help us change the future.*

Self-Validate

The second self-care issue is the ability to *self-validate*. This is the ability to recognize the efforts and changes you've implemented in your thinking, in your language and in your behavior, as well as the improvements you've been experiencing in your relationships. Conscious effort is required because, if you're like most people, you'll tend to focus on the times you blow up or mess up. Fine. Notice these things and allow them to help you chart a new course of action.

But let's keep the focus on what you're doing well. Keep a journal — a *positive* journal — to validate events such as:

- A day you got through without yelling or shaming
- A new motivation strategy you discovered
- A boundary you set successfully
- A need you communicated clearly
- An agreement you and your child negotiated peacefully
- A problem you listened to supportively
- A conflict you detached from quickly
- A behavior you acknowledged lovingly.

Honor the dedication and commitment that you demonstrated by reading this book and by any new behaviors you've tried along the way. Validate your willingness to self-examine and to change. These are no small accomplishments.

Go back and take the self-assessment test again in "How Do You Parent?" (Chapter 4). Has your thinking changed? Would you answer the questions the same way? Look over the old messages and new messages in "The Challenge of Setting Boundaries" (Chapter 2). Do the new messages sound as strange as they did the first time you encountered them?

Each of these is evidence of your growth, not just as a parent, but as a healthy, integrated individual. I congratulate you! If you do it for your kids, that's nice. One day they may even appreciate it. But I hope even more that you do it for yourself. No one is worth it more.

EXERCISE

List the characteristics of the people you need in your support network.

_____

_____

Identify someone you know who has these characteristics (or some place you can go to find people like this).

_____

_____

Identify three things you've done in the past week to take care of yourself.

1. _____
2. _____
3. _____

What are some other things you can do to take care of yourself? Feel free to add to this list any time a new idea strikes.

1. _____
2. _____
3. _____
4. _____
5. _____
6. _____
7. _____
8. _____
9. _____
10. _____

Start a positive journal — in the form of a notebook, a calendar or even a scratch pad — to keep track of what you're doing well on a daily basis. Wind up your day by writing down at least three things you did well each day. Do not use any qualifiers (e.g., "but," "only" or "except"). Just focus on the positive.

Duplicate the "Weekly Reflection" form below to use as a tool to validate your skills and track your growth each week.

Weekly Reflection

New strategies or behaviors I tried out this week.

_____

_____

_____

Something that went really well this week.

_____

_____

_____

Something I'll do differently next time.

_____

_____

_____

Evidence of growth in my own behavior.

_____

_____

_____

Evidence of improvements in my relationships with my children.

_____

_____

_____

My goals for next week.

_____

_____

_____

Thirty

In Closing

Okay, it's time for a metaphor. This process of building relationships is a journey. Wherever you are in your relationships with your kids, you didn't get there by accident and you didn't get there overnight. Whether the road's been smooth or bumpy, you now have the opportunity to develop new skills that will make the journey more pleasant for all concerned.

If you've come this far, it's obvious you have a pretty strong commitment to creating, or strengthening, the relationship you have with your children. Remember that for the rest of your life, no matter what happens, you are your children's parent. If you are looking forward to enjoying a long-term, loving relationship with them — whether or not you've put much into the foundation so far — now is a great time to start.

OBSTACLES TO SUCCESS

I personally applaud whatever excitement and enthusiasm you carry into this journey and would like to leave you with a few hints for avoiding the inevitable potholes you will encounter.

Problem Of Impatience

One of the greatest obstacles you may face is your own impatience. Let's face it, you've probably tried at least a few of these ideas at some point or another. If your past efforts didn't pay off the way you'd hoped, it may be because you didn't maintain the changes long enough. Remember, relationship-building takes time, especially in a relationship that's been plagued by conflict, misunderstanding and mistrust. Perhaps your greatest challenge will be trusting the process long enough to stick it out. Nothing will undermine your goals faster than the need for a quick fix.

How long will it take before you start seeing healthier and more loving behaviors? It's hard to say. Sometimes the simplest changes can produce dramatic results. On the other hand, it may take your kids a while to trust your commitment. Most parents report that their best results came when they were able to keep their focus on long-term goals and when they restrained the impulse to change every one of their bad habits before lunch.

Problem Of Perfectionism

Perfectionism will also derail your efforts, especially if initial changes don't end up being as permanent as you'd like. Relationships require continued effort and attention, but even well-tended relationships experience setbacks and trying times. A lapse into old patterns doesn't mean the process isn't working. Keep in mind that the process can be remarkably inconsistent. Some days you'll feel as if you're sliding back two steps for each step you take forward. Be careful that you don't give up on the entire journey just because you've stumbled along the way. (If you've ever completely blown a diet because of one extra bite, you know exactly what I'm talking about.)

Feeling It's Too Late

Another obstacle may be the feeling that you've waited too long. If you're having serious problems with your kids, you may have read through some of these chapters thinking, "Well, this may work for some families, but it's probably too late for us." *Do not despair.* The hill may look too steep to tackle, but it is possible to get to the top, although it may take some additional help and a little more time.

If your relationship is in serious trouble, start by identifying your needs, your resources and, if necessary, your legal rights and responsibilities. Build a strong support network of people who have information you need, who are emotionally available, who have been where you are and who can accept and love you unconditionally. Take action: Establish and communicate your boundaries and follow through. Leave the door open for your kids to change their minds. Let go. And in the meantime, *take care of yourself.* This, too, shall pass.

Lack Of Support

A lack of support from your spouse or parenting partner, other family members, neighbors or the school can erode your efforts as well. However, you improve your chances for getting support when you specify your goals and needs. But even if all else fails, you can continue to move forward on your path regardless of how other people in your children's lives behave. Maintain your boundaries, your commitment, your sobriety and your integrity — after all, this is your responsibility, although you don't have to do it alone. If your family won't support you, find people who will. Keep in mind that things usually get worse before they get better.

Daily Life

Finally, there are the more subtle obstacles that come in the form of distractions in daily life which can push relationship-building to the tail end of your priority list. Keep in touch with your commitment through daily self-validation activities, inspirational literature, tapes, affirmations, people or whatever little reminders will work for you.

(One parent took a few index cards and drew a big black plus sign on each one. He put one in his wallet, one in the car, one on the bathroom mirror and so on, just to remind himself to focus on the positive.)

Enjoy!

Enjoy the journey. Laugh, play and have fun together along the way. Check out the scenery. Watch out for potholes. And even though this may be the most important journey you ever make, don't forget to stop and smell the roses from time to time.

Related Reading

Alberti, Robert E. and Michael L. Emmons, **Your Perfect Right: A Guide To Assertive Living.** Impact Publishers, 1990.

Beattie, Melody, **Beyond Co-dependence.** Harper/Hazelden, 1989.

Beattie, Melody, **Co-dependent No More.** Harper/Hazelden, 1987.

Becnel, Barbara Cottman, **The Co-dependent Parent.** Harper-SanFrancisco, 1991.

Becnel, Barbara Cottman, **Parents Who Help Their Children Overcome Drugs.** CompCare Publishers, 1990.

Bloomfield, Harold, M.D., **Making Peace With Your Parents.** Ballantine Books, 1983.

Bluestein, Jane, Ph.D. and Lynn Collins, M.A., **Parents In A Pressure Cooker.** Modern Learning Press, 1989.

Bradshaw, John, **Bradshaw On: The Family.** Health Communications, 1988.

Bradshaw, John, **Creating Love.** Bantam Books, 1992.

Bradshaw, John, **Healing The Shame That Binds You.** Health Communications, 1988.

Bradshaw, John, **Homecoming.** Bantam Books, 1990.

Branden, Nathaniel, Ph.D., **Breaking Free.** Bantam Books, 1973.

Branden, Nathaniel, Ph.D., **Honoring The Self.** Bantam Books, 1983.

Branden, Nathaniel, Ph.D., **The Power Of Self-Esteem.** Health Communications, 1992.

Brondino, Jeanne, et al., **Raising Each Other: A Book For Parents And Teens.** Hunter House, 1988.

Buscaglia, Leo, Ph.D., **Living, Loving & Learning.** Fawcett, 1982.

Buscaglia, Leo, Ph.D., **Love.** Fawcett, 1972.

Buscaglia, Leo, Ph.D., **Loving Each Other.** Fawcett, 1984.

Buscaglia, Leo, Ph.D., **Personhood.** Fawcett, 1978.

Clarke, Jean Illsley and Connie Dawson, **Growing Up Again.** Harper/Hazelden, 1989.

Cline, Foster, M.D. and Jim Fay, **Parenting Teens With Love And Logic.** Pinon Press, 1992.

Cloud, Henry, Ph.D. and John Townsend, Ph.D. **Boundaries.** Zondervan Publishing House, 1992.

Cole, Jim, **The Controllers: A View Of Our Responsibility.** Growing Images, 1971.

Cole Jim, **The Facade: A View Of Ourselves.** Growing Images, 1990.

Cole, Jim, **The Helpers: A View Of Our Helplessness.** Growing Images, 1990.

Cole, Jim, **Thwarting Anger: A View Of How We Keep Anger Alive.** Growing Images, 1985.

Collins, Lynn, M.A. and Jane Bluestein, Ph.D., **Parents In A Pressure Cooker: Parent Workbook.** Modern Learning Press, 1989.

Dowling, Collette, **Perfect Women.** Summit Books, 1988.

Elchoness, Monete, Ph.D., **Teen Issues Workbook** (companion to **Why Can't Anyone Hear Me?**). Monroe Press, 1989.

Elchoness, Monte, Ph.D., **Why Can't Anyone Hear Me?** Monroe Press, 1989.

Elchoness, Monte, Ph.D., **Why Do Kids Need Feelings?** Monroe Press, 1992.

Faber, Adele and Elaine Mazlish, **How To Talk So Kids Will Listen & Listen So Kids Will Talk.** Avon Books, 1980.

Ginott, Dr. Haim, **Between Parent & Teenager.** Avon Books, 1969.

Glenn, H. Stephen and Jane Nelsen, Ph.D., **Raising Self-Reliant Children In A Self-Indulgent World: Seven Building Blocks For Developing Capable Young People.** Prima Publishing, 1988.

Goodman, Gerald, Ph.D., **The Talk Book: The Intimate Science Of Communicating In Close Relationships.** Rodale Press, 1988.

Harris, Thomas, M.D., **I'm O.K., You're O.K.** Avon Books, 1969.

Hart, Louise, Ph.D., **The Winning Family.** LifeSkills Press, 1990.

Hipp, Earl, **Fighting Invisible Tigers: A Stress Management Guide For Teens.** Free Spirit Press, 1985.

Jampolsky, Gerald G., M.D., **Love Is Letting Go Of Fear.** Bantam Books, 1981.

Jesse, Rosalie Cruise, Ph.D., **Healing The Hurt: Rebuilding Relationships With Your Children.** Johnson Institute, 1990.

Johnson, Kendall, Ph.D., **Turning Yourself Around: Self-Help Strategies For Troubled Teens.** Hunter House, 1992.

Johnson, Lee and Sue Kaiser Johnson, **If I Ran The Family.** Free Spirit Press, 1992.

Miller, Alice, **Banished Knowledge: Facing Childhood Injuries.** Doubleday, 1990.

Miller, Alice, **For Your Own Good: Hidden Cruelty In Child-Rearing And The Roots Of Violence.** Farrar, Straus, Giroux, 1984.

Miller, Alice, **Thou Shalt Not Be Aware: Society's Betrayal Of The Child.** Meridian Book, 1986.

Miller, Angelyn, **The Enabler: When Helping Harms The Ones You Love.** Hunter House, 1988.

Muller, Wayne, **Legacy Of The Heart.** Simon & Schuster, 1992.

Murdock, Marueen, **The Heroine's Journey: Women's Quest For Wholeness.** Shambhala Press, 1990.

Nelsen, Jane, **Clean And Sober Parenting.** Prima Publishing, 1992.

Nelsen, Jane, **Positive Discipline.** Ballantine Books, 1987.

Oliver-Diaz, Philip and Patricia A. O'Gorman, **12 Steps To Self-Parenting.** Health Communications, 1988.

Paul, Jordan, Ph.D. and Margaret Paul, Ph.D., **If You Really Loved Me.** CompCare, 1987.

Paul, Margaret, Ph.D., **Inner Bonding: Becoming A Loving Adult To Your Inner Child.** HarperCollins, 1990.

Porterfield, Kay Marie, **Keeping Promises: The Challenge Of A Sober Parent.** Hazelden Foundation, 1984.

Roberts, Gail C., M.A. and Lorraine Guttormson, M.A., **You And School.** Free Spirit Press, 1990.

Roberts, Gail C., M.A. and Lorraine Guttormson, M.A., **You And Stress.** Free Spirit Press, 1990.

Roberts, Gail C., M.A. and Lorraine Guttormson, M.A., **You And Your Family.** Free Spirit Press, 1990.

Rolfe, Randy Colton, **Adult Children Raising Children.** Health Communications, 1990.

Smith, Carol Cox, **Recovering Couples.** Bantam Books, 1992.

Subby, Robert, **Lost In The Shuffle: The Co-dependent Reality.** Health Communications, 1987.

Vedral, Joyce L., Ph.D., **My Parents Are Driving Me Crazy.** Ballantine Books, 1986.

Whitfield, Charles, **Healing The Child Within.** Health Communications, 1987.

Woititz, Janet G., Ed.D., **Healthy Parenting.** Fireside Books, 1992.

Youngs, Bettie B., Ph.D., Ed.D., **Safeguarding Your Teenagers From The Dragons Of Life: A Parent's Guide To The Adolescent Years.** Health Communications, 1993.

Important Books for Parents
from Health Communications

DAILY AFFIRMATIONS FOR PARENTS
How to Nurture Your Children And Renew Yourself
During The Ups And Downs Of Parenthood
Tian Dayton

If you're taking care of children and trying to care for yourself too, you deserve encouragement and loving ideas for keeping everyone's needs in perspective.
Code 151-8 .... $6.95

PEACEFUL PREGNANCY MEDITATIONS
A Diary For Expectant Mothers
Lisa Steele George

Affirmations for every day you're expecting cover the joys and fears of pregnancy. There's room to record your own feelings on each page.
Code 2638 .... $9.95

ENERGY SECRETS FOR TIRED MOTHERS ON THE RUN
B. Kaye Olson

This complete guide to protecting and renewing your energy resources tells how to manage your family and job and keep life in balance.
Code 2506 .... $11.95

HOW TO TURN YOUR MONEY LIFE AROUND
The Money Book For Women
Ruth Hayden

Feelings of fear and shame about money keep many women from taking charge of their finances. Help for developing appropriate attitudes and useful money skills.
Code 2255 .... $9.95

CHICKEN SOUP FOR THE SOUL
101 Stories to Open The Heart And Rekindle The Spirit
Jack Canfield and Mark Victor Hansen

Here is a treasury of 101 stories collected by two of America's best-loved inspirational speakers. Put a smile in your heart and share it with your family.
Code 262X $12.00

3201 S.W. 15th Street
Deerfield Beach, FL 33442-8190
1-800-851-9100

**Health
Communications, Inc.®**